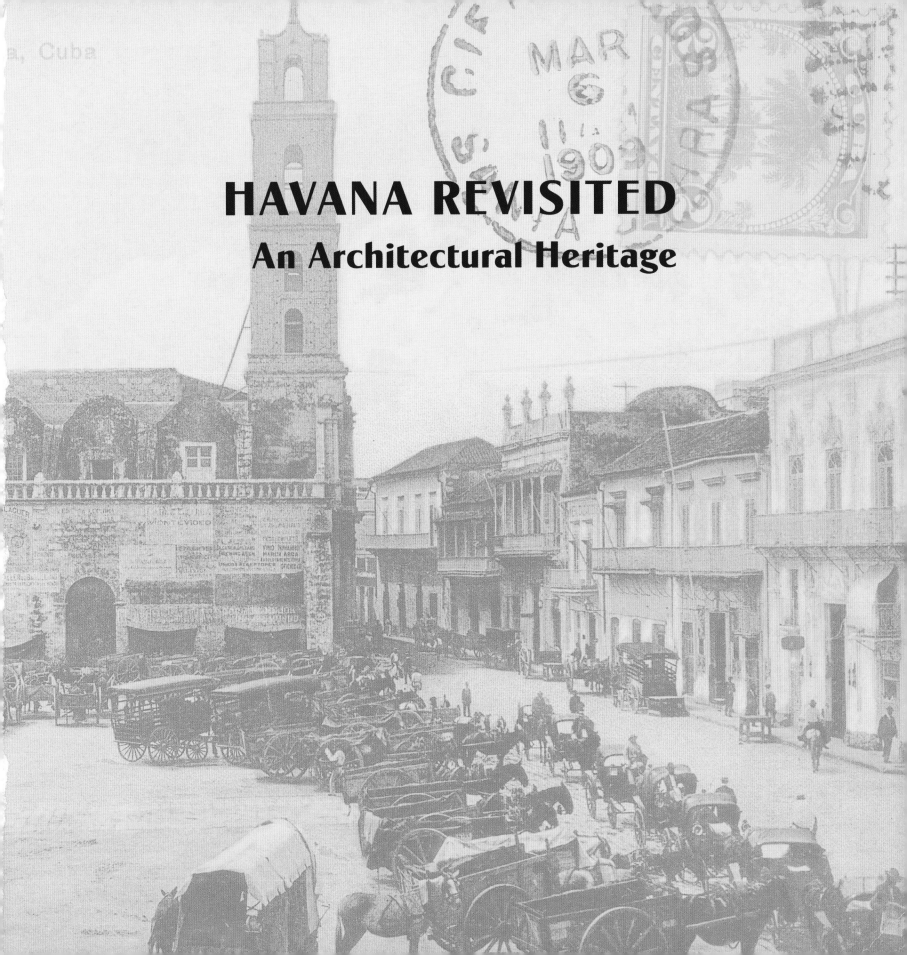

HAVANA REVISITED
An Architectural Heritage

HAVANA

REVISITED

An Architectural Heritage

CATHRYN GRIFFITH

TRANSLATIONS BY DICK CLUSTER

W. W. Norton & Company
New York • London

Copyright © 2010 by Cathryn Griffith

For information about permission to reproduce selections from
this book, write to Permissions, W. W. Norton & Company, Inc.,
500 Fifth Avenue, New York, NY 10110

For information about special discounts for bulk purchases,
please contact W. W. Norton Special Sales at
specialsales@wwnorton.com or 800-233-4830

Manufacturing by KHL Printing Co. Pte Ltd
Book design by Jonathan D. Lippincott
Production manager: Leeann Graham

Library of Congress Cataloging-in-Publication Data

Griffith, Cathryn.
  Havana revisited : an architectural heritage /
Cathryn Griffith ; translations by Dick Cluster. — 1st ed.
    p. cm.
  Includes bibliographical references and index.
  ISBN 978-0-393-73284-9 (hardcover)
1. Architecture—Cuba—Havana. 2. Historic buildings—
Conservation and restoration—Cuba—Havana. 3. Havana
(Cuba)—Buildings, structures, etc. I. Title.
  NA804.H3G75 2010
  720.97291'23—dc22
                                            2009031697

ISBN: 978-0-393-73284-9

W. W. Norton & Company, Inc.
500 Fifth Avenue, New York, N.Y. 10110
www.wwnorton.com

W. W. Norton & Company Ltd.
Castle House, 75/76 Wells Street, London W1T 3QT

0 9 8 7 6 5 4 3 2 1

Postcard publishers, where their names are given, are:

In Havana: Betancourt Hnos.; C. Jordi; Diamond News Co.;
Edición Jordi; Harris Bros. Co.; Lit Omega; Mario Guardiola;
Roberts & Co.; Roberts Tobacco Co.; Swan; and Torrea y Costa/
Campanario.

In the United States: Colourpicture Publication, Boston; Curt Teich
& Co., Inc., Chicago; Detroit Photographic Company; E. C. Kropp,
Milwaukee; Illus. Post Card Co., New York; The Rotograph Co.,
New York; H. H. Stratton, Chattanooga, Sunny Scenes, Inc., Win-
ter Park, Florida.

Photos by Todd Forsgren: pages 32 bottom, 33 bottom, 34 bottom,
35 right, 62 bottom, 95 right, 127 bottom, 130 bottom, 196 bottom.

Photo by Esley Pérez: page 189 bottom.

All other photographs are by the author.

CONTENTS

FOREWORD   Eusebio Leal Spengler   7

PREFACE AND ACKNOWLEDGMENTS   9

INTRODUCTION: HAVANA   Mario Coyula   13

MAP OF HAVANA   16

1. PLAZA DE ARMAS   Félix Julio Alfonso López   19

2. MORRO CASTLE AND THE FORTRESS OF THE CABAÑA   Silvia María Morales Pérez   39

3. PLAZA DE SAN FRANCISCO   Mario Coyula   55

4. PLAZA DE LA CATEDRAL AND ITS CHURCH   Daniel Taboada   71

5. CHURCHES AND CEMETERIES   Carlos Venegas Fornias   81

6. STREETS AND MARKETS   Orestes M. del Castillo   103

7. SIGNS OF THE TIMES: HAVANA'S REPUBLICAN LANDMARKS REVISITED
   Lillian Guerra   121

8. CAPITOLIO NACIONAL AND PARQUE CENTRAL   Mario Coyula   139

9. PASEO DEL PRADO   Leland Cott   161

10. MALECÓN   Mario Coyula   177

11. EL VEDADO   Pedro Contreras   201

12. ACROSS THE ALMENDARES   Felicia Chateloin   217

ABOUT THE CONTRIBUTORS   233

BIBLIOGRAPHY   235

INDEX   236

FOREWORD

Eusebio Leal Spengler

Alongside the Plaza de Armas, that historic space from which the city first spread, stands the old seat of government, the Palacio de los Capitanes Generales. From the year 1791 on, it served as the palace of the Spanish captains general and as the seat of Havana's local government.

Those well versed in Hispanic-American architecture are struck by the fact that the Plaza de Armas may be the only Plaza Mayor in the Americas not dominated by a cathedral. A glance through the entrance hall of this beautiful building reveals a wide courtyard of severe Spanish Renaissance inspiration—more precisely, Herrerian, the style named after the architect Juan de Herrera. In its modern version, the courtyard holds a garden which, like a tropical canopy flanked by two royal palms, surprises all who arrive.

It's a cool and murmuring courtyard, in which the song of the smallest bird may be heard, while trickles of water from the enormous cistern below enchant with their melodies. Filled with greens of subtle and varying hues that accent the moist Havana air, this perfumed garden invites us to refresh ourselves beneath the spacious arcades once enclosed by stained-glass windows or wooden lattices.

This is how we were, and this is how we are seen: seen by, for instance, the anonymous artists of the beautiful colored postcards now gathered in this lovely book, a nostalgic and—why not—romantic message from the marvelous and indescribable Havana.

(Opposite) The beautifully restored courtyard of the Palacio de los Capitanes Generales is home to a peacock and peahen. The sculpture of Christopher Columbus commemorates his landing on the island of Cuba on October 28, 1492, during his first voyage to the Americas.

7

PREFACE AND ACKNOWLEDGMENTS

The origins of this book date to April 2003, when I arrived in Havana for the first time. On the way from the airport to my hotel on Parque Central that Sunday afternoon, I was captivated: people sat talking in parks, while others walked along the streets, which were remarkably devoid of the automobile traffic I was used to seeing in American and European cities. Most of all, I noticed the urban spaces and architecture—streets, parks, and magnificent buildings. I wondered: Who designed them? When and for what purpose were they built? How are they used now?

A few months after that trip, I bought some picture postcards of Havana in a Paris flea market and determined to seek the locations when I returned to Cuba. My musings became a deepening curiosity, fed by the colorful old postcards I continued to collect. Since then, I have returned to Havana again and

again to look for the places illustrated in my growing collection, and I have begun to learn about the city and its history.

As the writers in this book recount, the so-called Spanish-American War resulted in Cuban independence from Spain in 1898. However, the United States remained deeply involved in Cuban affairs for years afterward, and during this period, large numbers of tourists from many countries, including the United States, visited Cuba.

Also during this period, picture postcards became a popular and affordable means of presenting images of a city to the world. Nearly two-thirds of the postcards reproduced in this book were never written on or mailed; most likely, they were cherished souvenirs of a visit to Havana in the days before travelers carried cameras. The postcards that were mailed went primarily to North and South America

HABANA. Central Park. — Parque Central.

The beauty of old postcards like the one above attracted me. In Havana, people were interested in the illustrations of bygone times and eager to help my assistant, Esley Pérez (on the left), identify the location of postcard pictures.

and Europe. In the absence of a dated message or postage cancellation, the style of the postcards is the most accurate guide to the approximate year they were printed. Early postcards had room on the front for a short message; the back was exclusively for the address. Beginning in 1907, the back accommodated both the address and the message, leaving the entire front for a picture. Postcards with a white border began appearing in 1915. And in 1930 a new process produced cards with a linen-like surface.

The postcard illustrations were derived from black-and-white photographs: a "colorist" cleaned up the image, conferring a blue sky and white clouds and often adding fanciful colors to produce a romanticized, appealing picture. Often the same image, with different coloration, appears on different cards.

All the postcards reproduced here were published in the United States or Cuba, and nearly all were made between 1900 and the early 1930s.

This book, on the other hand, is the product of twenty-first-century media and equipment. I purchased virtually all the postcards on the Internet. I took all the new photographs with a digital camera (unless otherwise noted).

As will become clear, some buildings have scarcely changed, some are badly decayed, and others are missing completely. Of the newly restored buildings, many were rebuilt from ruins by the Office of the Historian of the City of Havana. Perhaps the most significant change in the city is the abundance of shade trees—most welcome in this sunny climate.

I am enormously grateful to the many Cubans who welcomed me and encouraged me in my work. The first person I met in Havana, Juan Roilan Gil Fis, piqued my interest in the city's history by telling of cannon shots and English warships—part of a tremendously rich history I knew nothing about. The artist Noa and his wife, Elaine de la Torre, gave invaluable support, not least by introducing me to Alejandro Alonso and Pedro Contreras, both enthusiastic historians of the city's architecture who generously shared their knowledge. Eduardo Luis Rodríguez contributed in numerous ways, including identifying the location of postcard images of El Vedado and the areas across the Almendares River, many of which have changed beyond easy recognition. Jesús Magan explored the city with me, including one memorable excursion when we rode together in an open trailer pulled by his cousin on a motorcycle. Esley Pérez became my near-constant companion while I worked. He knocked on doors to seek access to people's apartments in order to photograph from their windows and balconies. The occupants were unfailingly gracious, and I acknowledge with gratitude Armando Rodríguez Pastor, Jesús de Sanluis Esposito, Carmen García, Jesús Gonzales Alvanos, Juana M. Tamayo, Ana Rivero, and Pablo Pérez Wong, as well as Padre Antonio Bendito at the Iglesia del Vedado. My loyal friends Clara Emilia Pérez and Martha Vega Quintana continue to enrich my understanding of Cuban culture and language.

I am deeply indebted to Lee Cott, the first American with whom I shared my vision for this book, and to Lillian Guerra, whom I first met in Havana, not only for their enthusiastic support but also for introducing me to their colleagues in Cuba. As a result, most of this book was written by renowned Cuban scholars, architects, preservationists, and urban planners. I am grateful for the vast knowledge these policy-makers, historians, and thinkers brought to the book and for their conscientious efforts to ensure its accuracy. It has been a pleasure to get to know them. Dick Cluster's extensive knowledge of Havana's history and infrastructure was as invaluable as his graceful style in translating the contributions written in Spanish.

My initial trips to Cuba were under a license granted to the School of the Museum of Fine Arts in Boston. Friends and supporters there include Maria Magdalena Campos-Pons, David Davison, Bonnie Donohue, Carl Sesto, and Chantal Zakari, each of whom provided ongoing encouragement and guidance as my project developed.

Derek Blackman, a life-long journalist and long-time friend, shared his observations of the city. Todd Forsgren accompanied me on one trip to make large-format photographs on film in an old-fashioned view camera. Others who contributed in significant ways are Mary Virginia Swanson, Jennifer Josten, Bonnie Leonard, Gary Chassman, Jerome Frank, and Dan Bornstein. Nancy Green, my editor, deserves highest praise for her patience and support, as well as for envisioning this book, which is more beautiful than I could have imagined. Nancy arranged her schedule so that we had the added pleasure of spending time together and meeting with the writers in Havana. Lastly, I thank my family, Sarah Griffith and Ray Lemieux, for their constant love and encouragement.

Habana: El Morro desde la Punta.
View of Morro from La Punta Fort.

INTRODUCTION: HAVANA

Mario Coyula

Havana's modest beginnings came in the sixteenth century, as the springboard for Spain's conquest of America. When the port became the obligatory last American stop for Spanish ships making their return voyages to Europe, its significance grew until Havana had become the most important city in the Gulf of Mexico and the Caribbean. From the beginning, it was a settlement oriented toward providing services, especially that of protection. Hence, Havana became home to the most formidable system of defensive fortifications in the colonial Americas.

Havana's urban design and architecture were more European than Caribbean in character. The mother country's influence remained stronger there than in any of the Spanish possessions on the continent, which won their independence eighty years earlier than Cuba. In addition, heavy Spanish immigration continued into the first quarter of the twentieth century, even more so than before independence (1898). These factors, together with the rapid disappearance of the native population and the proximity of the United States, made Havana more Spanish and also more North American.

The city grew by expansion, with little demolition or replacement in its older sections, and thus it accumulated valuable layers of distinct architectural periods and styles. These layers range from a lone example of Renaissance military architecture, the Castillo de la Real Fuerza (La Fuerza castle), constructed 1558–1577, the oldest fort built out of lasting materials by Europeans in America (see Chapter 1), to the seventeenth-century pre-Baroque with Mudéjar influence from southern Spain, the austere Cuban Baroque of the eighteenth and early nineteenth centuries, some examples of the Neo-

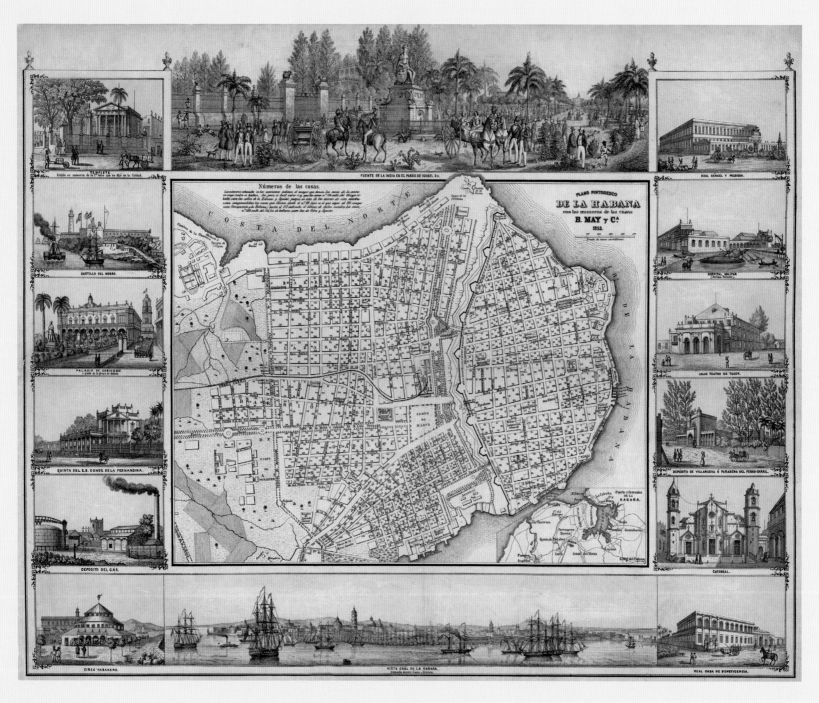

Gothic in the mid-nineteenth century, and the ubiquitous neoclassical style favored by the Cuban-born sugar aristocracy from the first third of the nineteenth century on. Toward the end of the eighteenth century, Havana had begun to acquire an image of elegance, supported by Cuba's burgeoning slave-based plantation economy. The capital expanded beyond its walls, gradually incorporating other small nearby settlements. Independent of all this extensive and valuable sixteenth-to-nineteenth-century colonial patrimony, however, the bulk of the city's twentieth-century building stock was created by and for a rising lower middle class. That growth spurt began with a brief period of Art Nouveau—really Catalan modernism—but is represented above all by the prevalent eclectic Beaux Arts, coinciding with an economic boom known as the "Years of the Fat Cows," which started during World War I and gave shape to the central areas of the capital and all the other cities of Cuba.

The original colonial Spanish city—with its layout of narrow streets, small and compact blocks, deep and narrow lots, and low buildings sharing common walls—expanded in the nineteenth and early twentieth centuries via the development of new areas like El Vedado (see Chapter 11), Santos Suárez, La Vibora, Lawton, and the western suburbs, all primarily residential. But those neighborhoods were built with tree-lined streets along which the buildings were detached from each other and separated from the sidewalks by front yards and private porches and porticos. Part of this pattern, too, were the so-called republican parks, tree-shaded plazas filling an entire square block each. In the beginning of the 1930s, the architecture that many would later call Art Deco reached Havana, at first in its geometric version and later the streamlined one. The architecture of the Modern Movement took some time to win acceptance but became dominant after World War II as part of the capital's second great twentieth-century construction wave. This history explains why most buildings in Havana are less than a hundred years old.

The bulk of the city's construction is made up of one- or two-story dwellings—the exceptions being some important public buildings, the condominium towers built in the 1950s, and the complexes of five-story walkup public housing built after 1959. The high design quality of 1950s architecture continued into the early years after the revolutionary victory of 1959, and was extended throughout the country and to new uses. The average level also improved. Later, excessive centralization and an emphasis on technological and quantitative aspects to the detriment of expressive ones—along with reduced diversity and a nullification of the personality of the designer—brought a loss of expressive quality in post-1960s Cuban architecture. Some special works managed to escape this tendency, but they were few and usually located in the city's periphery, so they had little impact on the urban image.

Havana's silhouette, rhythm, texture, character, and scale are very special. The city is low-slung but clearly urban, and its low density confers a special quality of life missing from Latin American cities that have suffered overdevelopment. The program of preservation, restoration, and rehabilitation of La Habana Vieja (Old Havana) and its fortifications, designated a World Heritage Site by UNESCO in 1982, has been notably successful, especially since acquiring independent financing mechanisms in 1993. At the dawning of the twenty-first century, Havana was a city where growth had not erased the imprints of the capital's many eras, and where inaction had contributed to preservation as well.

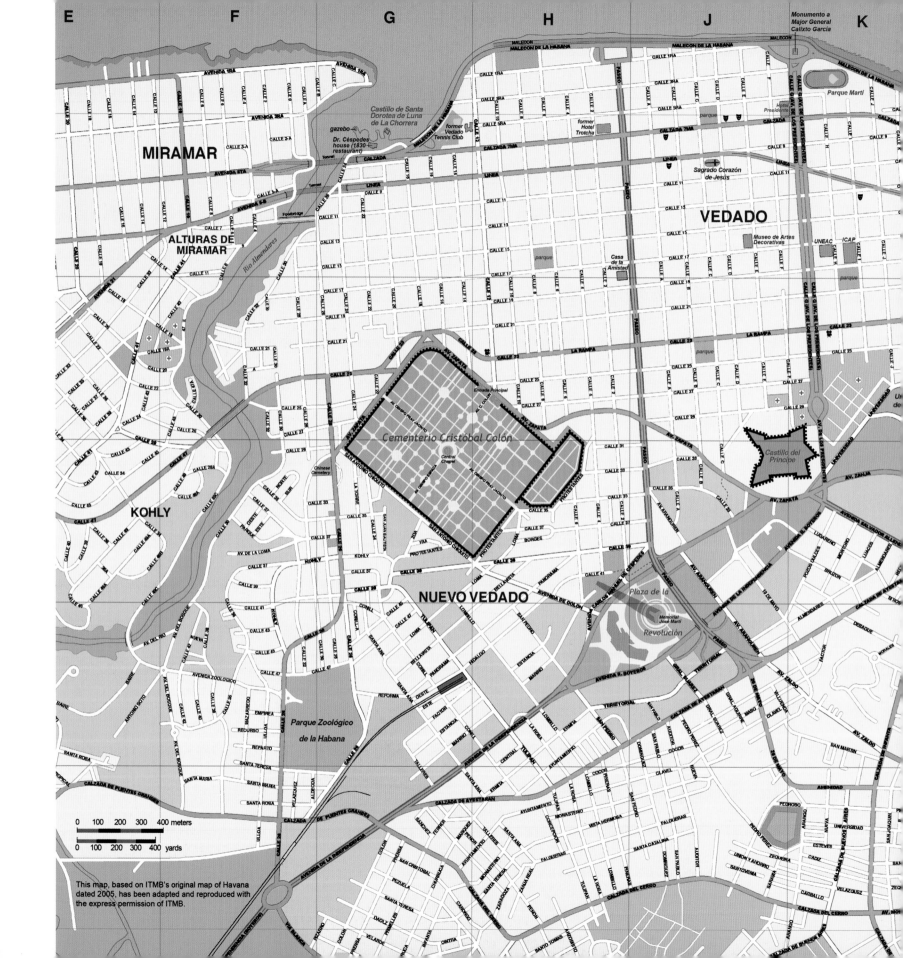

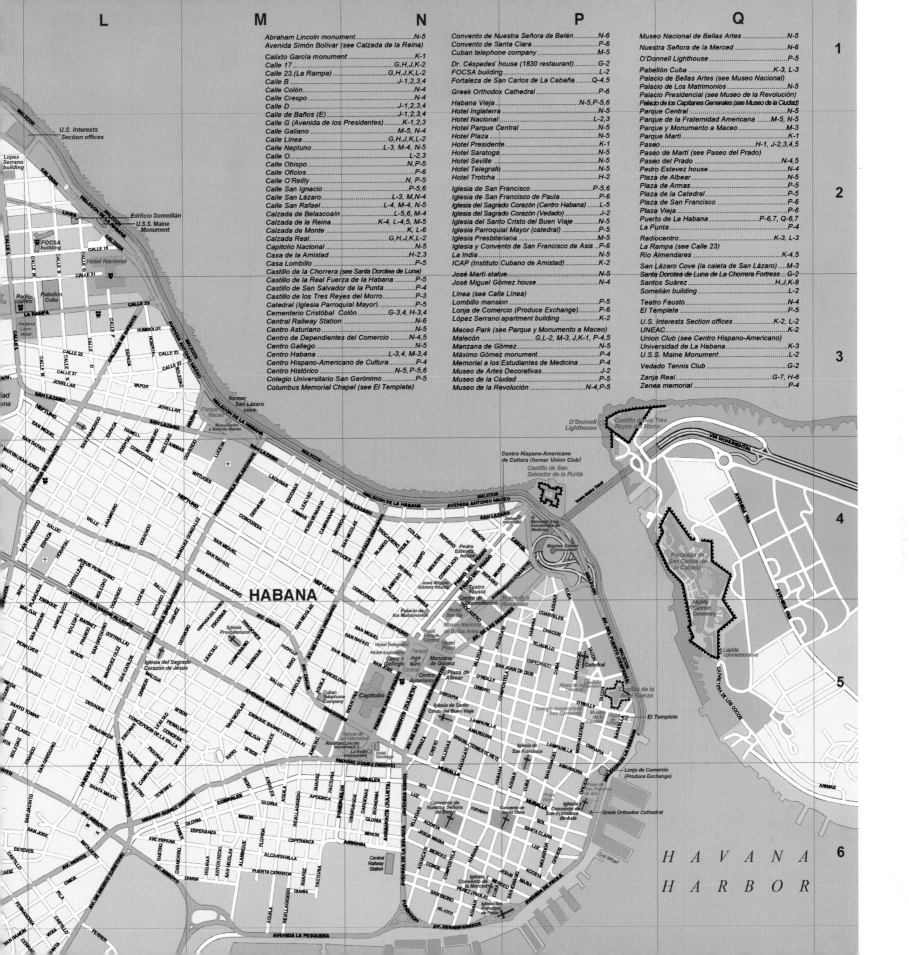

Abraham Lincoln monument................................N-5
Avenida Simón Bolívar (see Calzada de la Reina)
Calixto García monument....................................K-1
Calle 17...G,H,J,K-2
Calle 23.(La Rampa)..................................G,H,J,K,L-2
Calle B...J-1,2,3,4
Calle Colón..N-4
Calle Crespo..N-4
Calle D..J-1,2,3,4
Calle de Baños (E)......................................J-1,2,3,4
Calle G (Avenida de los Presidentes)............K-1,2,3
Calle Galiano..M-5, N-4
Calle Línea...G,H,J,K,L-2
Calle Neptuno.....................................L-3, M-4, N-5
Calle O...L-2,3
Calle Obispo...N,P-5
Calle Oficios..P-6
Calle O'Reilly..N, P-5
Calle San Ignacio..P-5,6
Calle San Lázaro.................................L-3, M,N-4
Calle San Rafael........................L-4, M-4, N-5
Calzada de Belascoaín.........................L-5,6, M-4
Calzada de la Reina........................K-4, L-4,5, M-5
Calzada de Monte.......................................K, L-6
Calzada Real...G,H,J,K,L-2
Capitolio Nacional...N-5
Casa de la Amistad..H-2,3
Casa Lombillo...P-5
Castillo de la Chorrera (see Santa Dorotea de Luna)
Castillo de la Real Fuerza de la Habana........P-5
Castillo de San Salvador de la Punta.............P-4
Castillo de los Tres Reyes del Morro..............P-3
Catedral (Iglesia Parroquial Mayor)...............P-5
Cementerio Cristóbal Colón.............G-3,4, H-3,4
Central Railway Station...................................N-6
Centro Asturiano..N-5
Centro de Dependientes del Comercio.........N-4,5
Centro Gallego...N-5
Centro Habana...............................L-3,4, M-3,4
Centro Hispano-Americano de Cultura.........P-4
Centro Histórico.......................N-5, P-5,6
Colegio Universitario San Gerónimo..............P-5
Columbus Memorial Chapel (see El Templete)

Convento de Nuestra Señora de Belén............N-6
Convento de Santa Clara..................................P-6
Cuban telephone company M-5
Dr. Céspedes' house (1830 restaurant)...........G-2
FOCSA building..L-2
Fortaleza de San Carlos de La Cabaña........Q-4,5
Greek Orthodox Cathedral P-6
Habana Vieja...............................N-5,6, P-5,6
Hotel Inglaterra...N-5
Hotel Nacional..L-2,3
Hotel Parque Central.......................................N-5
Hotel Plaza..N-5
Hotel Presidente..K-1
Hotel Saratoga...N-5
Hotel Seville..N-5
Hotel Telegrafo...N-5
Hotel Trotcha...H-2
Iglesia de San Francisco.............................P-5,6
Iglesia de San Francisco de Paula...................P-6
Iglesia del Sagrado Corazón (Centro Habana)...L-5
Iglesia del Sagrado Corazón (Vedado)............J-2
Iglesia del Santo Cristo del Buen Viaje..........N-5
Iglesia Parroquial Mayor (catedral)................P-5
Iglesia Presbiteriana.......................................M-5
Iglesia y Convento de San Francisco de Asís..P-6
La India..N-5
ICAP (Instituto Cubano de Amistad)..............K-2
José Martí statue...N-5
José Miguel Gómez house..................................N-4
Línea (see Calle Línea)
Lombillo mansion..P-5
Lonja de Comercio (Produce Exchange)..........P-6
López Serrano apartment building...................K-2
Maceo Park (see Parque y Monumento a Maceo)
Malecón.................G,L-2, M-3, J,K-1, P-4,5
Manzana de Gómez..N-5
Máximo Gómez monument...............................P-4
Memorial a los Estudiantes de Medicina........P-4
Museo de Artes Decorativas...........................J-2
Museo de la Ciudad...................................N-5, P-5
Museo de la Revolución..............................N-4, P-5

Museo Nacional de Bellas Artes N-5
Nuestra Señora de la Merced N-6
O'Donnell Lighthouse P-5
Pabellón Cuba..K-3, L-3
Palacio de Bellas Artes (see Museo Nacional)
Palacio de Los Matrimonios N-5
Palacio Presidencial (see Museo de la Revolución)
Palacio de los Capitanes Generales (see Museo de la Ciudad)
Parque Central..N-5
Parque de la Fraternidad Americana M-5, N-5
Parque y Monumento a Maceo......................M-3
Parque Marti...K-1
Paseo.......................................H-1, J-2,3,4,5
Paseo de Martí (see Paseo del Prado)
Paseo del Prado..N-4,5
Pedro Estevez house...N-4
Plaza de Albear...N-5
Plaza de Armas..P-5
Plaza de la Catedral...P-5
Plaza de San Francisco.......................................P-6
Plaza Vieja...P-6
Puerto de La Habana.........................P-6,7, Q-6,7
La Punta...P-4
Radiocentro...K-3, L-3
La Rampa (see Calle 23)
Río Almendares..K-4,5
San Lázaro Cove (la caleta de San Lázaro)....M-3
Santa Dorotea de Luna de La Chorrera Fortress..G-2
Santos Suárez..H,J,K-8
Somelián building...L-2
Teatro Fausto..N-4
El Templete...P-5
U.S. Interests Section offices...................K-2, L-2
UNEAC...K-2
Union Club (see Centro Hispano-Americano)
Universidad de La Habana.................................K-3
U.S.S. Maine Monument...................................L-2
Vedado Tennis Club...G-2
Zanja Real...G-7, H-6
Zenea memorial..P-4

HABANA

HAVANA
HARBOR

1

PLAZA DE ARMAS

Félix Julio Alfonso López

Unlike other important colonial cities of Spanish America—such as Mexico City, Lima, Quito, or Buenos Aires—Old Havana lacks a dominant central space around which all the main functions of civil, political, and religious life are clustered. In other words, there is no Plaza Mayor as such, surrounded by the government offices, the cathedral, and the town hall. Instead, those symbols of colonial power are distributed across a set of plazas that give the city an unusual polycentric character.

The Plaza de Armas could have been considered a Plaza Mayor in principle, because it was the site, in 1519, of the founding of the city of Havana in its permanent location, which took place at the foot of a leafy ceiba tree after two false starts elsewhere. However, the plaza began losing its attributes as a public space for festivals and markets from the sec-ond half of the sixteenth century on, as a result of the construction of the Castillo de la Real Fuerza (1558–77), on the seaward side of the plaza. The new fortress required moving the governor's residence, the town council offices, the jail, and the homes of some principal residents. The resulting space became the external grounds of the military citadel, good for drilling troops and for gathering residents in case of attack.[1]

In contrast with this defensive character of the Plaza de Armas, the Iglesia Parroquial Mayor (the major parish church) continued to coexist with the fort—in fact, the area had at some point been called the Plaza de la Iglesia—though without the missionary function that Catholic sanctuaries fulfilled in the plazas of other Spanish-American cities, since Havana lacked a large indigenous population. The governor of the colony, for his part,

1. Carlos Venegas Fornias, *Plazas de intramuro*. La Habana, Consejo Nacional de Patrimonio Cultural, 2003, p. 17.

19

HABANA:— CASTILLO DE LA FUERZA.

LA FUERZA FORT. (OLDEST BUILDING 1540.)

The Castillo de la Real Fuerza de la Habana is the oldest building in the city. The early Spanish governors lived here before the Governors' Palace was built, and the royal shield of the House of Austria, which ruled Spain at the time, is installed above the entrance. La Fuerza has served many uses, and presently is the Museum of Maritime History.

This is where I live at present

N.º 31 HABANA CASTILLO DE LA FUERZA.-«LA FUERZA» FORTRESS

Habana: La Fuerza, el Templete y la Cabaña al Fondo

La Fuerza Fort, Colombus Chapel and Cabana Fortress, Havana, Cuba

The Plaza de Armas is strategically situated at the entrance to Havana harbor, across from Morro Castle and the Fortress of the Cabaña. Freighters still arrive regularly, but cruise ships bring passengers to Havana far less frequently than in the years before air travel.

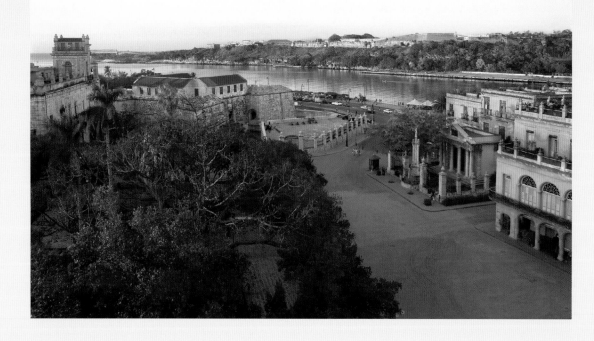

G 12086 Tower of La Fuerza (The oldest Fort in Habana)
Torre de La Fuerza (El Castillo mas antiguo de la Habana)

The watchtower, built as part of the fortification system protecting the Spanish colonial city, has become a well-known symbol of Havana. The bronze weathervane on the tower, called La Giraldilla de la Habana, is the figure of a woman holding a palm tree in her right hand and a cross in her left. The original, the oldest sculpture in Cuba, is in the Castillo de la Real Fuerza and a full-scale replica about 3 1/2 feet (1 meter) high sits atop the watchtower.

finally established his residence in the Castillo de la Real Fuerza, but the town hall remained itinerant for some time.

Still, over the course of the sixteenth and seventeenth centuries, the Plaza de Armas retained its status as the main square of the city by virtue of being surrounded by the fort, the church, a Dominican convent, a hospital, and a tree that was used for public floggings, as can be seen in a map of 1691 attributed to Juan de Síscara. But this preeminence would soon be challenged by new planned spaces like the Plaza Nueva, the Plaza de San Francisco (see Chapter 3), and the Plazuela de la Ciénaga (see Chapter 4).

By the second half of the eighteenth century, the historian José Martín Félix de Arrate deemed the Plaza de Armas "one of the three main squares" of the city, but judged its place in the hierarchy to be lower than that of the Plaza de San Francisco, "which is nearly the best site in the capital."[2] The church was damaged by the explosion of a ship in 1741, the ceiba was felled in 1753, and the plaza became relegated more and more to a space for reviewing and drilling troops. Its loss of symbolic importance and the lack of important buildings in the surrounding area are reflected by the fact that the English draftsman Elias Durnford ignored it in his series of engravings of the main plazas of the city during the British military occupation (1762–63).[3]

The modernizing impulses of enlightened despotism, represented in Havana by the government of Captain General Felipe Fondesviela, Marqués de la Torre (1771–76), turned new attention to the Plaza de Armas with the goal of converting it into a political-civic center of the first order where the main buildings representing the colonial power would stand.

This urban project, marked by the monumental scale of the Baroque, included demolition of the old church and its replacement by a majestic palace that would serve as the headquarters of the city administration, the jail, and the governor's residence. Known as the Palacio de los Capitanes Generales, it was built during the period 1776–91. A bit earlier, in 1771, on the adjoining side of the square between this site and the Real Fuerza, work had begun on the Casa de Correos (postal headquarters). Also called the Palacio del Segundo Cabo (second-in-command), it was judged in its time to be the island's architectural gem.

In the first decades of the nineteenth century, the Plaza de Armas continued to regain importance and status. The planting of a new ceiba tree and the addition in 1828 of Cuba's first neoclassical building, the commemorative El Templete, at the urging of Bishop Espada, restored the high symbolic content associated with the city's origins. The beautification and ornamentation projects carried out by the captains general Francisco Dionisio Vives (1823–32) and Miguel de Tacón (1834–38) transformed the plaza itself, replacing the harshness of its traditional military image with a space graced with paving stones, planted grounds, and benches—a spot appropriate for walking, meeting, or diversion.

When Spanish domination of Cuba ended in 1898, the Palacio de los Capitanes Generales witnessed the transfer of powers to the U.S. intervention authorities, who established headquarters there. Then it became the seat of power of the Republic until 1920. The city government continued to occupy part of the building until 1967, when reconstruction efforts began, leading to the building's present use as the Museo de la Ciudad (Museum of the City).

2. José Martín Félix de Arrate, *Llave del Nuevo Mundo. Antemural de las Indias Occidentales. La Habana descripta, noticias de us fundancíon, aumentos u estados.* La Habana, Comisión Nacional Cubana de la UNESCO, 1964, pp. 77–78.
3. Carlos Venegas Fornias, op. cit., p. 58; and Roberto Segre, *La Plaza de Armas de La Habana. Sinfonía urbana inconclusa.* La Habana, Letras Cubanas, p. 12.

CITY HALL, OLD SENATE AT RIGHT   7A148

(Above and on the following page) Postcards of the Plaza de Armas from the early 1900s show the Palacio de los Capitanes Generales and, at right, the Palacio del Segundo Cabo, later the Senate. The views show many changes in the formal plantings, but in every case the absence of established shade trees exposed the pathways to the burning Caribbean sun. Today, the square is covered with a canopy of leaves, providing a cool resting place for people to gather and talk.

Félix Julio Alfonso López   25

HABANA: PLAZA DE ARMAS, AYUNTAMIENTO

CITY HALL AND SENATE BUILDING

122611

PRESIDENT'S PALACE, Havana, Cuba.

27   PUBL. BY DIAMOND NEWS CO. HAVANA.

COACH STAND NEAR THE PALACE.

Presidents' Palace, Havana, Cuba

A life-size sculpture in the center of the Plaza de Armas faces the harbor, with the Palacio de los Capitanes Generales (Governors' Palace) behind.

The Senate of the Republic occupied the Palacio del Segundo Cabo until the completion of the Capitolio Nacional in 1929, while the National Archive and the National Library each occupied the Castillo de la Fuerza at various times. Facing a third side of the plaza was the embassy of the United States.

In 1923, thanks to the initiative of Emilio Roig de Leuchsenring, the city historian, the plaza was renamed Carlos Manuel de Céspedes. This was a prelude to a long process of replacing the statue of the Spanish king Fernando VII with one of Céspedes, the Cuban patriot regarded as the father of his country. Of the restorations carried out during this time, the most important was that of the Palacio de los Capitanes Generales in 1930, by the architects Evelio Govantes and Félix Cabarrocas. Two basic aspects of this work stand out. Inside, the upper-floor galleries overlooking the courtyard were finished, thus

HAVANA: COLUMBUS MEMORIAL CHAPEL

El Templete, or Columbus Memorial Chapel, faces the Plaza de Armas and houses three wall-to-ceiling oil paintings by the French artist Jean Baptiste Vernay depicting the first Mass, the first town council meeting, and the inauguration of the Templete. The three-sided column in front, erected in 1754, is believed to mark the place where the settlement called San Cristóbal de la Habana was founded in 1519.

HABANA.
El Templete.
Colombus
Memorial
Chapel.

Habana.

No. 216. Wilson's Obispo 52. Habana.

Salon de recibo de Palacio. — Drawing room of the Palace.

This impressive reception hall on the second floor of the former Governors' Palace overlooks the plaza. Between 1791 and 1898, the palace was home to sixty-five governors of Spanish colonial Cuba. Immediately after the Spanish-American War, it served as the seat of the United States government. Rededicated as the Museum of the City of Havana in 1967, the building is open to the public.

G 12003 The Palace Courtyard - Patio del Palacio, Habana.

Arched colonnades rise on all sides of the courtyard of the Governors' Palace, festooned with palms, bougainvillea, and other tropical foliage. A marble statue of Christopher Columbus, by the Italian J. Cuchiari, has ornamented the courtyard since 1861.

12005 The Palace Colonnade - Columnata del Palacio, Habana.

Having a good time. Dewitt.

A long portico supported by Ionic columns on the ground level of the palace provides protection from sun and rain. At the request of one of the governors, wood was used to pave the street in front of the palace to soften the noise of passing carriages.

G 12004 The Palace Entrance - Entrada del Palacio, Habana.

completing the original plan of a patio surrounded on all sides by walkways above. Outside, the colored plaster that had long ago been applied to the external walls was removed to expose the original sea-formed limestone beneath. Many other details were repaired at the same time: walls, ceilings, floors, stairways, carpentry, and electric wiring. The monument to Columbus, which had adorned the center of the courtyard since 1862, was also restored. In 1935, in the plaza itself, Emilio Vasconcelos redid

Removal of the stucco façade in 1930 altered the appearance of the palace by exposing the limestone beneath.

the furniture and gardens to match their appearance in nineteenth-century prints.

In recent decades, restoration work carried out by the Office of the Historian of the City of Havana has restored the plaza to its old splendor, converted the palaces and castles into museums and cultural centers, and put the old mansions to use as tourist facilities or community services such as libraries and art galleries. To all this we must add the people who gather in the park and its environs: the booksellers whose stands add a cultured note to the borders of the plaza, the city's residents who come every day to talk beneath the shade of palms and bougainvilleas, and all those who flock here on November 16 for the ritual circling of the ceiba, in the hope that their fondest wishes will be fulfilled.

(Opposite page left) The annual celebration of the founding of Havana, held on November 16, attracts throngs of people who wait in line for hours to take their turn walking around the ceiba tree in front of La Templete as they make a wish for the coming year.

(Opposite page right) A fashion show in front of the Palacio de los Capitanes Generales holds the attention of a large crowd, including uniformed security guards in the courtyard and on the balcony.

(This page top) Booksellers display many old books about Cuban history and Cuban heroes.

(This page bottom) Band concerts are another popular activity in the Plaza de Armas. A variety of music is performed, including American show tunes.

2

MORRO CASTLE AND THE FORTRESS OF THE CABAÑA

Silvia María Morales Pérez

The town of San Cristóbal de la Habana was founded at its current location on the Bay of Carenas in 1519. Five years earlier, in 1514, Captain Pánfilo de Narváez and Friar Bartolomé de las Casas had founded a town of the same name on Cuba's southern coast, of which no traces now remain. The northern location offered not only a far superior bay and harbor—one of the most important in the Caribbean—but also the shelter provided by the rocky promontory known as La Cabaña, which gave protection from the hurricanes that frequently lashed the island. This location also served as a jumping-off point for the conquest of new territories.

From these earliest sixteenth-century years, however, Havana faced periodic sieges by privateers and pirates. Between 1538 and 1543, the attacks came from French privateers, of whom the most famous was Jean-François de la Roque, the Seigneur de Roberval. Later, in 1555, Jacques de Sores left the town in ruins, overcoming defenders in the so-called Old Fort, a rough and never-completed stronghold of mostly uncut stone. De Sores's raid demonstrated the urgent need for improved defense and security, which led to the building of the first permanent fortress with true military bastions. Constructed from 1558 to 1577 under the supervision of master builder Francisco de Calona, the Castillo de la Real Fuerza had one major drawback: its location well inside the neck of the bay condemned it to limited usefulness.

Still facing frequent attacks by enemy fleets, (those of Holland and England as well as France), Spanish authorities next created what is known in hindsight as the city's first defense system, of which the Castillo de los Tres Reyes del Morro (castle of the three kings of the *morro*) is one of the most

Habana: El Morro desde la Punta.
View of Morro from La Punta Fort.

Habaneros enjoy the view across the harbor from Havana toward the Morro.

representative works. The name stems from the fort's geographic position, the term *morro* designating a high, isolated, rocky seaside cliff. Guards had been posted on this site as early as 1553, and in 1563, during the governorship of Captain Diego de Mazariegos (1556–65), a watchtower about 39 feet (12 meters) in height had been built, improving the vantage point of the lookouts and serving as a landmark for Spanish ships approaching the bay. On December 26, 1589, the first stone of Morro Castle itself was set in place by its designer, the Italian engineer Bautista Antonelli, and Governor Juan de Tejeda (1589–94).

The design of the new fortress featured a military enclave perfectly fitted to the irregular terrain. Its polygonal form with obtuse angles permitted defense

HABANA, EL MORRO DESDE LA CABANA

MORRO CASTLE FROM CABANA FORTRESS

1B-H607

This view from La Cabaña looks toward the lighthouse and the harbor entrance.

Silvia María Morales Pérez   41

GULF AVENUE FROM MORRO CASTLE   1B-H606

Morro Castle welcomes tourists during the day and, during the evening, often hosts a disco where Cubans relax in the cool air.

from any attack by sea, while a dry moat approximately 70 feet (21 meters) deep provided a difficult obstacle for an enemy attempting to enter the castle by land. The immense walls topped with battlements were fabricated out of cut and shaped stone to withstand enemy cannon fire. Interior spaces within the polygon were perfectly connected so as to facilitate the movement of the defending troops. Storerooms, barracks, offices, dungeons, and a church were all included, as well as cisterns for water storage.

Work on the Morro continued into the seventeenth century, when the fortress was officially inaugurated around 1615 under the governorship of Gaspar Ruiz de Pereda. It successfully defended the harbor and the city until 1762, when the English managed to capture Havana. At that time, the Morro revealed its weaknesses in relation to advances in the art of war. Its steep walls were too exposed to the enemy, and its strategic position was undercut by the proximity of La Cabaña hill, from which the English attackers, after forty-four days of siege, succeeded in taking the castle.

After the British occupation ended, in accordance with the terms of the Treaty of Paris, Spanish authorities made changes in the formal structure of the Morro. Between 1763 and 1766, an inner building was designed to be explosive-proof, while platforms for longer-range cannon batteries (such as the one called La Reina, the queen) were added. The old lookout tower was rebuilt; but not until the following century, when it finally collapsed, did the lighthouse we see today appear. Known as the O'Donnell Lighthouse after Governor Leopoldo O'Donnell (1843–48), who promoted its construction, it was activated in the mid-nineteenth century. Built to one side of the

Habana: Farola del Morro.
Lighthouse in Morro Castle.

original location, the new tower measured 16 feet (5 meters) in diameter and 98 feet (30 meters) high.

Near the castle, on the same height from which the English had succeeded in capturing the city, the Fortaleza de San Carlos de la Cabaña formed a key part of the second defense system of the city, render-ing one of the most vulnerable parts of the capital secure. Designed by the engineer Silvestre Abarca, begun in 1763, and finished in 1774, it was named in honor of Spain's King Carlos III and took its place as one of the most important military construc-tions in the Americas. With walls of cut stone like

The lighthouse, bearing the date 1844, serves as a beacon for arriving ships and is a distinctive landmark when seen from the city.

12091 Entrance to Fort Cabanas - Entrada al Fuerta de la Cabaña.

those of the Morro but nearly hidden behind great earthen slopes, La Cabaña could withstand the most advanced weaponry.

Like the Morro, the new fortress was polygonal in shape, resembling a pointed crown, was protected by a wide moat, and featured ample parade grounds inside. Its several sections are linked by avenues, ramps, and courtyards. One may still walk today through the wide vaulted rooms that served as barracks. The system of tunnels and other advanced technology gave it a very modern character for its epoch. Stretching nearly 2,300 feet (700 meters) along its strategic position east of the city, La Cabaña occupies twenty-five acres of terrain.

This impressive gate marks the entrance to La Cabaña.

N.º 26   HABANA LÁPIDA CONMEMORATIVA EN LA CABAÑA.
MEMORIAL OF CUBAN SHOT IN CABAÑA

This rarely visited memorial is located in a isolated area of La Cabaña.

PANORAMA OF CABAÑA FORTRESS.

Cannon and other defense
elements have been
preserved at La Cabaña.

Silvia María Morales Pérez   47

This vast fortification naturally required a huge investment (14 million pesos in gold), which gave rise to a famous anecdote in which the king, in Madrid, is said to have demanded a telescope so as to "see such a fantastic construction" for himself. The majestic fortress marked a change in the construction concept of the Havana fortifications, influenced by the French theories of the Marquis de Vauban and adapted to Caribbean geographic conditions. Its walls, crowning the entrance to the bay alongside the Morro, were never put to the test.

Having left behind their defensive character, today the two enclosures form parts of the Morro-Cabaña Military Historical Park, a tourist attraction that allows visitors to explore and admire each of the spaces and to enjoy the exceptional views of the Havana skyline that they provide.

8266. BOAT LANDING BENEATH CABANAS, HAVANA, CUBA.   COPYRIGHT, 1904, BY DETROIT PHOTOGRAPHIC CO.

The Morro and La Cabaña were previously reached by small boats. Now they are accessible via the four-lane Havana Harbor Tunnel, built by the Cuban government in 1958.

The cannons at Morro Castle protected the harbor and city of Havana.

This elaborate portal leads into the former chapel, known as La Capilla de la Fortaleza de San Carlos de La Cabaña.

Nightly at 9:00 P.M., young soldiers dressed in uniforms similar to those worn by officers and soldiers during the reign of Carlos III parade to a cannon overlooking the harbor, where they fire a single shot. This tradition, dating from the eighteenth century, originally signaled the closing of Havana's city gates. The ceremony still carries important historical meaning for Havana residents, who gather at La Cabaña or along the edge of the bay to listen and watch for the shot.

Silvia María Morales Pérez   49

Habana:
Vista desde Casa Blanca.
View from Casa Blanca

In this view from La Cabaña toward Havana, the Castillo de la Real Fuerza de la Habana—the oldest fortification in Havana—is visible at the far left.

HABANA Vista desde la Cabaña. View from Cabanas Castle

The dome of the Produce Exchange in the Plaza de San Francisco, across the harbor, can be seen in the postcard and recent photo.

The Church and Convent of San Francisco de Asis dominate one side of the Plaza de San Francisco. Members of the Franciscan order were established in Havana as early as 1570.

3

PLAZA DE SAN FRANCISCO

Mario Coyula

The name of this plaza comes from the old Church and Convent of San Francisco de Asis (St. Francis of Assisi), constructed 1719–38. This very important complex includes the second-highest colonial bell tower in Cuba as well as a lovely entrance to the church from Calle Oficios in the form of a splayed arch with concentric telescoped molding. An interesting architectural detail visible in the lateral façade of the church, which forms the south side of the plaza, is the way the five roof vaults built to admit light join with the barrel vault that covers the main nave. The dome that once roofed the crossing of the church's transept and nave was destroyed in 1850. When the sanctuary was rebuilt in 1994, a trompe l'oeil painting was commissioned to depict this vanished dome from inside. The first cloister of the convent was restored in 1996, and the second in 1998. Because of its excellent acoustics, the decon-secrated church now serves as a concert venue for classical music, while the galleries and rooms of the convent's large cloisters host exhibitions and scholarly events.

An area where rubble was cleared from behind the church, facing the Avenida del Puerto, became in 1998 a beautiful garden dedicated to Mother Teresa of Calcutta. In 2002, the area next to this garden became the site of a reinterpretation of a Greek Orthodox church, constructed almost in miniature, beautiful as well but controversial because of its lack of authenticity, especially in this locale. Rehabilitation of the historical complex—under the supervision of the dean of Cuban restoration architects, Daniel Taboada, throughout the process—was completed by restoration of the Chapel of the Third Order in 2005. Facing the main entrance to the church on Oficios are two artists' galleries in beautiful houses of

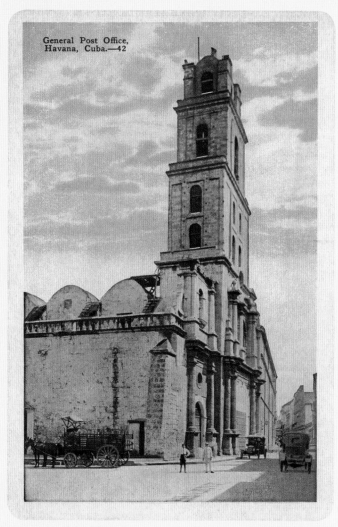

General Post Office,
Havana, Cuba.—42

After the English occupation
in 1762, which occurred
during the Seven Years' War,
the Spanish considered the
church impure. It served as
a post office for many years,
before the restoration of the
Plaza de San Francisco and
the surrounding buildings.

colonial-period aristocrats, now also restored. One of them includes the studio of Nelson Domínguez, among the major contemporary Cuban painters.

In spite of the strong presence of the church and convent, the Plaza de San Francisco is also tightly tied to the history of the port. As early as 1628, the site was set aside as a staging area for supplying the ships of the Spanish fleet, thus defining its com-

mercial character. That character was reinforced in 1909 by construction of the beautiful Lonja de Comercio (Produce Exchange) building, whose dome is crowned by a bronze statue of Mercury, god of commerce. Designed by the architect Tomás Mur, it was one of the first office buildings in the city. In 1996 it was remodeled according to a design by the Spanish architects Eduardo de Villegas and Javier

Custom House and Square, Havana, Cuba

General Post Office, Havana, Cuba.

Erected as a Catholic Church, over 250 years ago.

The royal palm is the Cuban national tree. The two tallest royal palms in the city are in the second cloister of the Convento de San Francisco, where they have grown tall searching for the sun.

The trompe l'oeil wall painting in the recent photograph gives the impression of a complete chancel and apse when, as can be seen from the uneven floor dimensions, this end of the church was truncated.

The Greek Orthodox Cathedral of San Nicolás de Mira, the first religious structure to be built in Cuba in 43 years, was dedicated on January 25, 2004. The Office of the City Historian provided the site and constructed the building in the garden behind San Francisco de Asis convent. The Greek Orthodox Church donated iconography and sacramental elements. There are a few thousand Orthodox Christians in Cuba, of whom only about fifty are Greek Orthodox.

The Caballero de Paris (The Gentleman from Paris) was a popular street person in the mid-twentieth century. An educated and gentle man distinguished by his long, unkempt hair and black cloak, he greeted passersby and discussed philosophy. This sculpture, created in his memory by José Villa Soberón, stands near the entrance to San Francisco church. The sculpture's beard and hand are shiny from being rubbed for good luck.

HABANA. — Machina landing harbour.
Muelle de la Machina.

This device, known as La Machina, was used to load and unload cargo. The tower of San Francisco church and convent appears in the background, showing the proximity of the Plaza de San Francisco to commercial activity in the harbor.

LUZ WHARF, HAVANA.

Wharf activity included small boats, as well as cargo and naval vessels.

4013. Produce Exchange, Havana, Cuba.

The Lonja de Comercio (Produce Exchange) was restored in 1995–96, when floors were added that partly obscure the view of the dome. Now a modern office building, it houses Havana Radio on the top floors.

HABANA: LONJA DEL COMERCIO Y ADUANA.

PRODUCE EXCHANGE AND CUSTOM HOUSE.

69525

Because of its proximity to the harbor and wharves, the Plaza de San Francisco was a center of commercial activity. More recently, until the plaza was restored, it served as a parking lot.

The small custom house stood in the busy commercial plaza, in front of the newer Luz warehouse where the customs office is now located. The reverse of this card reads:

The Lace Store
Real Spanish hand-made laces, mantillas, handkerchiefs, fans, all kinds embroidered and drawn work dresses, collars, bedspreads, table covers, center pieces and fillet laces.
97 Obispo St. – Havana
Every body speak English here.
Suarez & Hno.

No 12~Plaza de San Francisco. Habana   Saint Francisco Square. Havana

CUSTOM HOUSE, SAN FRANCISCO WHARF.

González de Adalid, under the technical direction of the Cuban architect Orestes del Castillo. Atypically for Havana, the Lonja is physically separated from the other buildings surrounding the plaza and situated at an angle to them. The Customs House, which marks the eastern edge of the plaza, was inaugurated in 1914 and included the offices of the inspector general of the port and the immigration authorities. Designed by the U.S. architectural firm Barclay, Parsons & Klapp, with a length of some 330 feet (more than 100 meters), it defines the eastern side of the plaza and almost completely blocks any view of the bay. The three towers of its façade, whose tile roofs probably reflect a desire for a colonial appearance, each correspond to one of the three piers behind. The building bears a curious

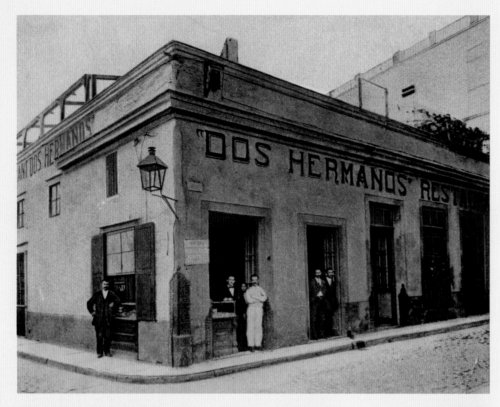

This bar has stood near the Plaza de San Francisco and the harbor for many years.

resemblance to the Embarcadero in San Francisco, California, perhaps inspired by the name of the plaza. In 1996, the pier closest to the mouth of the bay was remodeled to serve as a cruise ship terminal, as designed by the Italian architect Alessandro Mensa. Across from the southernmost of the three towers stands the Dos Hermanos bar, much patronized by sailors. The bar was originally named, in English, Two Brothers.

The irregular shape of the Plaza de San Francisco is unusual in Hispano-American design. Also, unlike the other main squares of Havana, this plaza is not surrounded by colonnaded passageways because the arcaded entrance of the Lonja de Comercio forms part of the building, not part of the urban public space. Approaching this plaza along Oficios from the Plaza de Armas, one comes first to a small open space in the form of an elongated triangle that joins the main plaza as a sort of vestibule, in a minor version of the Venetian tradition of piazza and piazzetta. In 1965, the lovely Fuente de Los Leones (Fountain of the Lions), the work of Giuseppe Gaggini, was restored to the center of the main plaza. This fountain had been donated in 1836 to the city by the Conde (Count) de Villanueva, who in 1837 established the first railway in Cuba, the seventh in the world. A Cuban-born aristocrat, Villanueva competed with the Spanish governor Miguel de Tacón in endowing works to improve and beautify the city.

Habana: Fuente de Los Leones. Capitolio 23

Havana: Lions Fountain, Capitol

The Fuente de Los Leones (Fountain of the Lions) was moved from Fraternity Park, near the Capitolio Nacional, to the Plaza de San Francisco in 1965.

The reverse of this card reads:
This artistic fountain stands at the Fraternity Square in the opposite side of La India fountain. The Fraternity Square with its gardens and marble monuments presents a colonial style very pleasant to the mind as all artistic things, and our Dr. Cespedes happily combined Beauty and Utility making this place fit for modern transit.

HABANA. FUENTE DE LOS LEONES

LIONS FOUNTAIN   123538

The Plaza de San Francisco attracts residents and tourists alike. Here, you can hire a horse-drawn carriage for sightseeing, watch a passing carnival troupe, pose for photographs with colorfully dressed cigar-smoking women, or simply sit and enjoy the beauty of the place.

HABANA.
Alrededores de la Catedral.
Vicinity of Cathedral.

The narrow side street next to the cathedral leads directly into the large plaza, which lies ahead and to the left.

4

PLAZA DE LA CATEDRAL AND ITS CHURCH

Daniel Taboada

A low-lying, swampy area subject to frequent flooding, this plaza remained on the fringes of the early growth of the town of San Cristóbal de La Habana, which clustered around the Plaza de Armas and the Plaza de San Francisco. Yet it came, in time, to be emblematic of the city, an obligatory spot on the itinerary of visiting Cubans and foreigners alike.

The square's unhealthy conditions were responsible for its first name, bestowed in the seventeenth century: Plazuela de la Ciénaga (swamp). A primitive spring provided barely enough water for neighboring houses and ships waiting in port. Then a branch of the Zanja Real (Royal Ditch) arrived, bringing a guaranteed supply of fresh water to a public bathhouse on the adjoining Callejón del Chorro. The area changed further in the eighteenth century thanks to the ups and downs of the Jesuit order, which in 1748 had begun building a church for its seminary on the corner of San Ignacio and Empedrado but in 1767 was expelled from the Spanish empire by King Carlos III. Left behind and unfinished by its originators, the church building was turned to use in 1772 as the city's main church, the Parroquial Mayor, after demolition of the church in the Plaza de Armas (see Chapter 1). Construction was completed in 1777, and formal dedication as the Cathedral of Havana followed in 1788. From then on, the square was known as the Plaza de la Catedral. The owners of the surrounding houses redesigned their dwellings so as to front on this now-desirable space, improving its perimeter with their new façades.

During religious festivals, the new plaza offered a fine location for the equally new colonial aristocracy to show off their carriages pulled by thoroughbred horses driven by black slaves, the so-called

Habana: Portales de la Plaza Catedral

Porches at Cathedral Square, Havana, Cuba

9A-H2190

The Lombillo mansion, occupied primarily by the Office of the Historian of the City of Havana, contains an art gallery on the ground floor, accessible from the porches.

caleseros. Succeeding eras brought further change. The center of the plaza at one time featured a tall gas lamp of simple design. Later came a light post that emerged from a circular fountain, each of its two arms ending in a frosted-glass globe with an electric bulb inside; the fountain, meanwhile, served as a watering trough for horses and mules. Another light post rose directly out of the ground, with two long curved arms from which globes of glass hung, and a spigot or spout for water alongside. The square itself was merely hard-packed earth at first, then cobblestones, later granite paving stones, and finally in 1930 it was redesigned with today's large granite blocks by Jean-Claude Nicolas Forestier, the noted French urban planner. Postcards show a lane around the outside enclosing a grassy center, but this may have been a colorist's invention. Other postcards show electric lines along the sidewalk traversing the arcades that front the mansions of the Marqués de Arcos and the Conde de Lombillo. The most

(Below and following page) This series of postcards shows the evolution of the Plaza de la Catedral.

The Cathedral.   Havana.

4002. Cathedral, Havana, Cuba.

Habana: Plaza de la Catedral.
          Cathedral Square.

Columbus Cathedral, Havana, Cuba.

HABANA: LA CATEDRAL.

THE CATHEDRAL.   106619

74   PLAZA DE LA CATEDRAL AND ITS CHURCH

noticeable change, in about 1935, was the removal of decorative plaster from the walls of these mansions and that of the Condes de Casa Bayona, which left the original stone exposed.

The Lombillo home—to the left of an observer standing in front of the church—had to be enlarged to match its predecessor and neighbor when the Marqueses de Arcos next door added their own new façade. Facing the cathedral from across the plaza is the mansion of the Condes de Casa Bayona, older than any of the others but lacking the shaded arcade with which they expanded their presence. Where

The paved Plaza de la Catedral, surrounded by stone buildings, is a popular gathering spot for Cubans and visitors alike. The bougainvillea on the Lombillo mansion provides a colorful touch of nature.

the Calle San Ignacio meets the dead-end Callejón del Chorro stands the mansion of Antonio Abad y Valdés-Navarrete, of imposing appearance with a splendid Baroque doorway. Known as the Casa de Baños, its 1935 neocolonial design harmonizes with the priceless antique buildings on all sides. Next door, the mansion of the Marqueses de Aguas Claras has an arcade facing the plaza, though it does not display the typical entranceway for carriages or the open inner courtyard to which a passageway would lead. Across the Calle Empedrado, we find the small palace built by the family of the Condes de San Fer-

nando de Peñalver, progenitors of many of the titled families of the colonial oligarchy.

The cathedral itself has an exceptional façade in the form of a massive altarpiece made up of three parts, each two sections in height, matching the three naves of the church. Its mixture of curves and straight lines incorporates characteristic Jesuit consoles and a round four-lobed window. The niches and scrollwork cornices exemplify the Baroque character of this architectural monument, unique in its era, whose fame has spread worldwide. The two austere towers rising on either side of the front

The paved Plaza de la Catedral, surrounded by stone buildings, is a popular gathering spot for Cubans and visitors alike. The bougainvillea on the Lombillo mansion provides a colorful touch of nature.

On a warm afternoon, tourists stop to enjoy a cool drink, to smoke a Cuban cigar, or to consult their guidebooks. Behind them is the mansion of the Counts of Casa Bayona, which today houses the Museo de Arte Colonial.

The mansion of the Marqueses de Aguas Clara, on the right, is presently a café. The three-story building to the left is the Casa de Baños, so-named because it formerly contained public baths.

HABANA. Interior of the Cathedral. — Interior de la Catedral.

The cathedral, which has been in continuous use for Catholic worship since it was built, retains the modifications made for the pope's visit in 1998.

form a striking contrast with this elaborate façade. A low balustrade that originally enclosed the raised entranceway was first removed but then finally restored in 1935.

In 1950, at the urging of Cardinal Manuel Arteaga, new modifications were made under

the direction of the architect Cristóbal Martínez Márquez. The original wooden pointed roof covered with clay tiles and hidden by a false ceiling was replaced by vaults and a stonework dome above the crossing. The remains of Christopher Columbus—discoverer of America and bearer

of Christianity—were once in the Cathedral of Havana, contained in an ornate and majestic sepulcher. When the Spanish left in 1898, they took with them the sepulcher and remains, which now rest in the Cathedral of Seville.

The visit of Pope John Paul II in 1998 required a final round of modifications to create a physically superior position for the throne where the pontiff would sit. The existing neoclassical small temple of marble from the nineteenth century had to be moved to the side chapel of Our Lady of Loreto, and the ancient Baroque choir with its central seat and niche restructured, thus sparing the sacristy any aggressive disturbance of that handsome space still furnished in the style of the eighteenth century. Havana's cathedral is the only Cuban example cited in the *Atlas of World Baroque*, compiled in 1994 by the UNESCO project "The Spaces of the Baroque." It is characterized by both "strength and agility," permanent attributes independent of human will.

The Plaza de la Catedral and its café remain a center of activity into the evening hours.

Iglesia del Santo Cristo del Buen Viaje (on Villegas between Teniente Rey and Lamparilla) is one of the city's most representative examples of Baroque style. Its façade was rebuilt of stone between 1733 and 1752. Typical motifs, such as vaulted arches and polygonal towers with characteristic finials, appear in a version devoid of the overwhelming decoration that generally characterized this style. Originally, the walls were plastered over with mortar and then painted as they appear in the postcard. The combination of a Baroque stone façade and an interior topped by wooden Mudéjar ceilings distinguishes this church, mixing materials and styles that usually do not appear together.

5

CHURCHES AND CEMETERIES

Carlos Venegas Fornias

Havana's churches have long served as examples of the city's unique architecture and customs. At the beginning of the twentieth century, the existence of a group of Catholic sanctuaries within what had once been the walled city affirmed Havana's long past as a Spanish colonial capital, but this older presence was succeeded by the newer Catholic churches, schools, asylums, convents, and monasteries dispersed throughout the growing barrios of the city. In addition, space opened up for buildings erected by Protestant denominations. Prohibited until the end of the nineteenth century within all the possessions of Spain, Protestant religions flourished in Cuba during the U.S. intervention (1898–1902).

The panorama of religious buildings shown here may be divided into two main groups: the colonial churches, convents, and monasteries of La Habana Vieja, almost all from the eighteenth century, and other newer ones built in various medieval revival forms that were called *estilos de devoción*. Studies of Havana's architecture classify the first within the colonial Baroque style, and the second within the "Neo-styles," or historicist architecture, especially the Neo-Gothic. The first constitute testimonials to tradition, while the latter point to a modernized and universalized presence.

The Church of Santo Cristo del Buen Viaje (Christ of the Good Journey) had been erected in 1640 as a small chapel on what was then the outer edge of the city, where three large crosses marked the endpoint of the Via Crucis, or Way of the Cross, a Lenten reenactment of Jesus' path to Calvary introduced by Franciscan friars. The church served worshipers of the Cristo del Buen Viaje, whose origin was the same. In 1903, the building was taken over

Iglesia de San Francisco de Paula (Paula between San Pedro and San Ignacio) was transformed in the eighteenth century into a stone sanctuary in the same style of sober decoration and Baroque design as Santo Cristo del Buen Viaje, as can be seen in the wide bell gable and in the undulating lines of the vault and the polygonal tower supporting the dome.

by a community of Augustine friars from Villanova College, near Philadelphia. They opened a grammar and secondary school alongside, with a specialty in English language classes.

The uses of the church of the women's hospital of San Francisco de Paula followed a similar path. Built in 1666 as the hospital chapel, it was reconstructed in its current form between 1731 and 1735 by the bishop and friar Lazo de la Vega. Urban progress took its toll in 1907 when the Havana Central Railroad Company demolished the hospital to expand tracks running to the nearby wharves. The church remained, secularized and isolated and awaiting demolition, as can be seen in the corresponding postcard. In 1945, however, it was declared a national monument and recently was restored and converted into a concert hall.

The building that housed the Convent of Santa Clara, the oldest existing in the city, also took on civil functions. As the city rose higher and higher above the convent walls, the resident nuns found it inadequate for cloistered life, and so they left it in 1922. The same story was repeated with other cloistered convents, whose orders likewise emigrated to newer neighborhoods in search of privacy.

The interiors of Havana churches were very modest in comparison with the sanctuaries of other Ibero-American colonies, never boasting a great volume of gilded altarpieces. In this sense, the more recent altars of churches like Nuestra Señora de la Merced and Iglesia de San Francisco came a little late to satisfy demands for more sumptuous decoration. In the first half of the nineteenth century, both churches were affected by liberal Spanish politics and the decloistering of religious orders. The

SANTA CLARA CONVENT, HAVANA, CUBA

Construction of a cloister of the Convent of Santa Clara (Cuba between Sol and Luz) began in 1638, and expansion continued until the first decades of the next century, when it included three cloisters and a vegetable garden. In 1925 it was taken over by the Department of Public Works, which transformed the patio of the main cloister into one of the most serene spaces in La Habana Vieja. It houses the Centro de Restauración Museológica and is also used for concerts and exhibition space and a small hotel.

Carlos Venegas Fornias   83

The main altarpiece of the church of Nuestra Señora de la Merced (corner of Cuba and Merced), inaugurated in 1867, was built by the architect José María Sardá from a design by the priest Ramón Querol. It is unique in allowing access by way of two lateral staircases to the anteroom of the Virgin of Mercy, a small chamber behind the altar that allowed parishioners to worship the carved image close up.

ALTAR OF SAN FRANCISCO CHURCH.   106642

former had belonged to the Mercedarian Order, who left it still unfinished a century after its inauguration, when the order was suppressed by the Spanish government. In 1863, the government gave the building to the Paulist Fathers, also known as the Congregación de la Misión. They transformed the church into one of the most elegant in the city: by 1874 they had spent a million pesetas on its reconstruction, a sum equal to about $200,000 at the time. The Franciscans, meanwhile, were similarly suppressed but returned around 1896 to occupy the former church of the Augustinians. This was demolished in 1919, and six years later they finished building a new sanctuary whose main altar featured a marble and plaster altarpiece holding antique and much-venerated images such as the Veracruz Christ.

The Iglesia de San Francisco (corner of Cuba and Amargura) occupied the site of the monastery of San Augustín, which dated from 1630. The Franciscans rebuilt it and opened it for services in 1925 with a new altar, shown here.

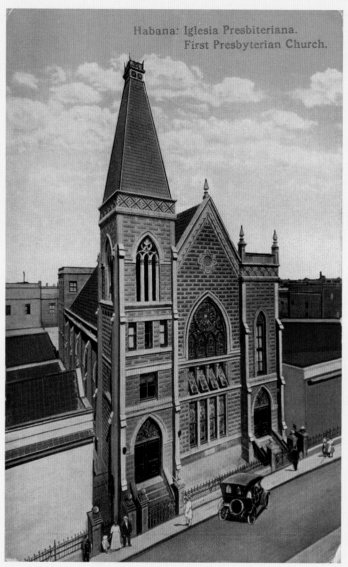

Habana: Iglesia Presbiteriana.
First Presbyterian Church.

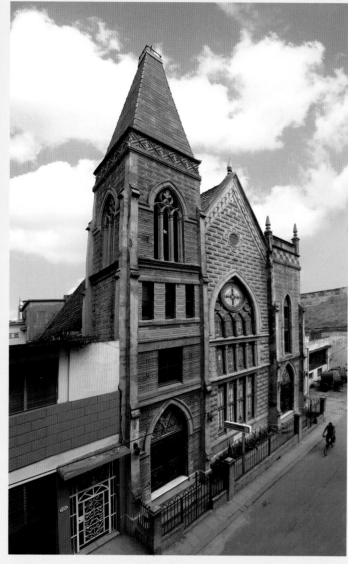

The Presbyterian Church (Salud between Lealtad and Campanario) was the first Protestant church built in the city, in 1906, and is still in use.

The Protestant faiths began the twentieth century with two buildings notable for their fidelity to historic styles, both in very central locations. In 1906, the Presbyterians opened a church in the northern Gothic style on Calle Salud, while for the Episcopalians, U.S. architect Bertram Grosvenor Goodhue designed the Cathedral of the Santísima Trinidad (Holy Trinity) under the influence of Mexican Baroque, especially its most Rococo variety (Churrigueresque, a style represented by José de Churriguera, a Spanish architect of the seventeenth and eighteenth centuries).

HABANA: IGLESIA PRESBITERIANA DE LA TRINIDAD.

HOLY TRINITY CHURCH.

106669

Construction of the Episcopal Church of the Holy Trinity (corner of Neptuno and Águila) began in 1907. The congregation moved to a new location in 1946 and the building was razed. On the site of the church is an apartment building with grocery store and hardware store on the ground floor.

Carlos Venegas Fornias 89

Habana: Iglesia del Vedado.
Vedado Church.

Catholic congregations, meanwhile, kept adding to their series of Neo-Gothic churches that had begun in 1871 with the reconstruction of Santo Ángel Custodio in La Habana Vieja. In 1912, the church of the Sagrado Corazón de Jesús (Sacred Heart) in Vedado was completed. The worship of the Sacred Heart was widespread in Cuba, having been spread by the Jesuits since the mid-nineteenth century, and it was that order which built the most splendid church of the city, also named Sagrado Corazón de Jesús, on the Calzada de la Reina in Centro Habana. This church is regarded as the most perfect example of the Gothic style in Havana. Its tower, 253 feet (77 meters) high, was designed by Brother Luís Gogorza in imitation of the cathedral in his native city of Burgos.

Construction of Iglesia del Vedado (corner of Línea and C) was approved in 1892 and completed in 1912. The bell tower was damaged by the hurricane of 1926 and rebuilt in 1931. The church is still in use.

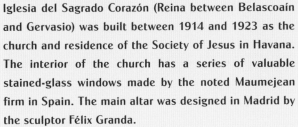

Iglesia del Sagrado Corazón (Reina between Belascoaín and Gervasio) was built between 1914 and 1923 as the church and residence of the Society of Jesus in Havana. The interior of the church has a series of valuable stained-glass windows made by the noted Maumejean firm in Spain. The main altar was designed in Madrid by the sculptor Félix Granda.

The Cementerio Espada, named for the bishop who commissioned it in 1804, was the first public cemetery in Cuba. French architect Étienne-Sulpice Hallet designed the cemetery, introducing the neoclassical style in Havana. A few burial vaults are still visible near San Lázaro Street.

Funerary rites had extraordinary importance in Havana from the sixteenth century onward. At the outset of the nineteenth century, for reasons of public hygiene, religious authorities prohibited the custom of burying the dead inside churches, and the resulting transfer of remains to the cemeteries gave rise to luxurious parades called *entierros* (burials) that wound through the city.

The antique cemetery of the city, the Cementerio Espada, was located within the expanding urban area, raising issues of hygiene and of space limitations as the city's population grew. In 1871, the Diocese of Havana began construction of a new cemetery in Vedado, which spread over 130 acres (53 hectares) according to a design by the architect Calixto de Loira. The gates of this Cementerio de Colón (Columbus Cemetery)—lodged in a triumphal arch of monumental Roman-Byzantine style—opened to the public in 1878. In 1904, the arch was crowned by a sculpture group entitled *Janua sum Pacis* (I am the

No. 11. Entrance to Colon Cemetery.
Entrada del Cementerio "Colón",
Habana, Cuba

best love Mary

The construction and style of the main gate of the Cementerio de Colón (Zapata and 12) were specified in the cemetery plan of 1870 by Calixto de Loira, but not completed until 1886.

Carlos Venegas Fornias   93

HAVANA: INTERIOR OF COLUMBUS CEMETERY

OB-H1128

The first section of the main avenue of the cemetery contains family mausoleums.

doorway to peace), the work of the Cuban sculptor José Vilalta de Saavedra, then living in Rome.

Within the broad expanse of the Cementerio de Colón, mausoleums and chapels of almost every architectural style are concentrated along the main "streets," which also display many Italian marble statues. The demand gave rise to enterprises known as *marmolerías*, which dedicated themselves to importing marble or finished sculptures from Italy, or to making sculptures on order in their own

workshops. In the twentieth century, the 50,000 tombs of the cemetery displayed such a great variety of sculpture—equally variable in quality—that tourists frequently remarked on its abundance and concentration.

Some of the mausoleums memorialized important social events. A monument to the medical students unjustly executed by a firing squad of Spanish vigilantes in 1871, for instance, was completed in 1890. Another monument of great value,

HABANA: PANTEON DE LOS ESTUDIANTES.

STUDENTS' TOMB.
69494

(This page and following page) This monument in memory of eight medical students unjustly shot by Spanish troops in 1871 was sculpted in Carrara marble by José Vilalta de Saavedra, who later made the sculptures for the main gate of the cemetery. The memorial was dedicated in 1890.

FIREMAN MONUMENT, Havana, Cuba.

8 PUBL. BY DIAMOND NEWS CO. HAVANA

dating to 1897, is dedicated to a group of firemen who died in a tragic accident.

Beyond its spreading grounds sown with tombs, the cemetery offered visitors two other attractions. One was Tobias's Gallery, an underground structure created for provisional burials while the cemetery was still being laid out; it made use of niches in a stepped design similar to an old catacomb. The other was the bone pile, an impressive open-air site for the skeletons of those who had no tombs and whose remains were not collected by relatives or friends. These bones played the classic *memento mori* role, recalling the fleetingness of life, just as the sepulchers and memorial tablets that surrounded the faithful in the old churches had done.

Foreign visitors also marveled at the luxurious

Sculptor Agustín Querol and architect Julio M. Zapata, both Spaniards, won the competition for the design of this monument, dedicated in 1897 to firefighters who perished in 1891 during a blaze in the Isasi hardware store.

Colon Cemetery Catacombs, Havana, Cuba.

The first burials took place in the catacombs of the cemetery, called Galería de Tobías (Tobias's Gallery). They are still in use today, more crowded than before.

funeral carriages pulled by horses with antique saddles and coachmen in livery and tricornered hats. The automobile eventually displaced this custom we now see only in old photos, but the importance granted to the rites of death, like all well-rooted traditions, sought new channels of expression within the dynamic river of modernity.

In scenes of the bone pile in 1902, groups of soldiers from the U.S. army of occupation, accompanied by Cuban guides in the lower picture, entertain themselves with the skeletons. The site of the former bone pile is now planted with grass and palm trees.

Funeral coach horses here are adorned in white. The color of the funeral train was not chosen arbitrarily. White indicated purity and was considered appropriate for children and unmarried women.

G 12082   A Cuban Hearse - Una carro de muerte.

In the early years of the twentieth century, a funeral proceeds up the Calzada de Reina toward the Cementerio de Colón.

749   REINA ST. FUNERAL PROCESSION, HAVANA, CUBA.   ILLUST. POST CARD CO., N. Y.

The chapel was designed in the same style as the front gate and erected in the middle of the cemetery between 1883 and 1885. The elaborate funeral coaches of a century ago have been replaced by contemporary motor vehicles. In the recent photograph, a coffin draped in the Cuban flag is being carried into the cemetery's chapel to receive a Catholic blessing.

Habana: Coche fúnebre.
Funeral Car. Cemetery Church.

DEMOLISHING OF THE OLD CITY WALL,
with view of the Church of „Angels", Havana, Cuba.

19   PUBL. BY DIAMOND NEWS CO. HAVANA.

The city walls that
surrounded La Habana Vieja
were demolished over a
period of years, beginning
in 1863. Many of the stones
were taken piece by piece
and used in the construction
of new buildings.

STREETS AND MARKETS

Orestes M. del Castillo

The Centro Histórico, part of Old Havana, exudes a special charm in its streets and commercial areas that has survived through time and difficulties to retain a most unique and striking character. This area consists of the Centro Histórico proper—the original urban space once surrounded by a large defensive wall—plus the territorial addition called Reparto de las Murallas (Walls District), created by the nineteenth-century demolition of that important fortification.

One interesting corridor, formed by the parallel streets named O'Reilly and Obispo, has lately been regaining its old liveliness. Many stores are newly reopened, some selling their accustomed wares of the past while others have new functions, but almost all are keeping traditions alive, not least by retaining their original names.

Obispo and some of its cross streets—Cuba,

Aguiar, Habana—contained Havana's banking and financial district, which is why the capital's residents, not without pretension, referred to this sector as "Little Wall Street." Nor can the Andalusian influence in our city be denied, as in the narrow streets long ago covered with awnings stretched from sidewalk to sidewalk like those of the Calle Sierpes in Seville, to offer welcome shade to the passersby.

From the olden images reflected in the antique postcards to the vibrant modern Centro Histórico captured in recent photographs, we can find continuity in the swirl and sounds of the human torrent flowing through these urban arteries. Where better to appreciate this than up and down Obispo, lately converted into a pedestrian walkway along its entire length, from the arcade of the Hotel Santa Isabel close by the sea to the tiny Plaza de Albear, which holds the marble image of the brilliant Francisco

Most of Havana is laid out on a grid pattern. This corner, unusual because of the sharp angle of intersecting streets, appears on many old postcards.

The Colegio Universitario San Gerónimo de La Habana is housed in a building of late twentieth-century construction. Its tower, when seen from this view looking up O'Reilly Street from the porch of the Palacio del Segundo Cabo in the Plaza de Armas, closely resembles the tower pictured in the old postcard.

G 12022a.   Empedrado St. - Calle de Empedrado, Cuba.

Recent excavations near the site of this photograph have been left open to reveal traces of the old city wall. Empedrado Street is in the city's historic center, an area of 500 acres (202 hectares) with 60,000 inhabitants. La Habana Vieja, which includes the historic center, encompasses a much larger area.

4007.   O'Reilly Street, Havana, Cuba.

A shop on O'Reilly, one of the principal shopping streets, advertised in the early 1900s that it sold *Antiquities and Curiosities, Works of Art, Cameos, Corals, Enamelled Goods, Filagree Jewelry, Tortoise Shell Objects, Feather Work* and other goods "at reasonable prices."

E 12018 Obispo Street - Calle Obispo, Habana.

The cables across
the shopping streets
held canopies that
shaded pedestrians
while also advertising
the shops.

G 12019a. Albear Square - Plaza de Albear, Habana, Cuba. *arrived this a.m. having a good time weather not stay here a week - Love - Bootsie -*

Francisco de Albear (1816–1887) was a Cuban-born engineer and general who designed several important public works, including the aqueduct that supplies Havana with water. This statue by Jose Vilalta de Saavedra of Albear in military uniform was dedicated in 1895.

Almendares optical shop is one of the most distinctive on Obispo Street.

A bakery displays a tempting variety of breads and pastries.

The decorated window glass of this store contributes an unusual architectural detail.

Decorated columns and elaborate stained glass distinguish this store that sells works by Cuban artisans.

Drogueria Johnson, an old-fashioned pharmacy containing dark wooden shelves filled with white porcelain apothecary jars, is being restored after a fire in 2006.

La Moderna Poesía (the Modern Poetry) building is a landmark at the top of Obispo Street near the Plaza de Albear.

de Albear y Fernández de Lara who, in his own right, can be considered one of the fathers of Cuban engineering.

Obispo is lined with stores, display windows, and names that are a permanent evocation of the originals. La Moderna Poesía, with its marvelous books, is now restored. There are the optical shop El Almendares, the department store La Francia with a new commercial twist, and the Hotel Florida reborn with its old name in what even earlier had been the mansion of Joaquín Gómez. There is the emblematic pharmacy complex made up of the Droguería Johnson and the Farmacia Taquechel, and some blocks

away the oldest and largest of all, the beautifully restored La Reunión pharmacy at the intersection of Compostela and Teniente Rey streets.

What can we say of the Belén Arch, which curves above a stretch of Acosta between Compostela and Picota? The arch adjoins the old monastery and convalescent hospital founded by the Bethlemite Friars. Later it was an important Jesuit school, where from his observatory Padre Viñas carried out his historic research on the hurricane systems that so affected the Cuban archipelago. That old arch, like so much in the Centro Histórico, has gained a new lease on life thanks

The marble paving stones of the Plaza Vieja reveal the outline of the Mercado de Cristina (Christina's Market) that formerly stood in the plaza.

Tacón market, one of the most active in the city, is no longer in existence.

G 12044 Habana - Street Scene,
Escena en una calle de la Habana

The Museo Nacional de Bellas Artes (National Museum of Fine Arts) is dedicated to work by Cuban artists. The stone arches flanking the entrance are thought to remain from the Mercado de Colón (Columbus Market) that previously stood on this site.

This market, El Mercado, is situated outside the old city, near the Ferrocarril del Oeste (train station to the west).

Merchants in El Mercado sell live poultry and meat, as well as fruits and vegetables.

to the wave of renovation which, little by little, is rescuing the past through an infusion of new energy.

Alongside the streets and shops, we cannot forget the markets. Some have left a trace. The contours of the old Mercado de Cristina may be seen in the marble paving stones of the Plaza Vieja. The Mercado de Colón has contributed two of its arches to the renovated Palacio de Bellas Artes. Others, more temporary, left no lasting footprints, but new markets have emerged to enliven the Centro Histórico. Multicolored crafts displays radiate out from the Plaza de la Catedral. In the stands around the Plaza de Armas, "almost any book on earth" may be found.

There are other elements, too, of the direct and living contact between buyer and seller: the elegant

In El Mercado, orange peels hang above a man who cranks a machine that prepares the oranges for eating, turning the peels into long tendrils.

An enterprising vendor pushes a wagonload of bananas through the streets of Old Havana.

Fruits and vegetables are abundant in this old view of an unidentified market.

An outdoor market serves a neighborhood in Centro Habana.

It is not unusual to see someone carrying a beautifully decorated cake through the city streets.

El Palais Royal, PELETERIA, AMERICAN SHOE STORE, La Casa de Moda, Obispo y Villegas.

8273. STREET CORNER MERCHANT, HAVANA, CUBA.

The old kiosk functioned as a small store; the new one, in the Plaza Vieja, provides cultural information.

kiosks of old Havana have reappeared in a new, green version in many convenient spots.

Such is the physiognomy of streets and shopping in the Centro Histórico of Havana, which lends its flavor as well to other expressions of the city's life in the public space. From the heights of their stilts, interpreters of the liveliest rhythms of the Cuban tradition amaze the passersby, while other dancers, from their own garden or taking the streets by storm, show off the purest contemporary moves.

116   STREETS AND MARKETS

Habana: Comparsa de Carnaval.
Carnival Scene.

Carnival performers who walk the streets of Havana's historic center daily are continuing a long-standing tradition of this form of entertainment in Cuba.

Habana: Comparsa de Carnaval.
Carnival Scene.

4016. Central R. R. Station, Havana, Cuba.

The Central Railway Station, designed by American architect Kenneth Murchison, was completed in 1912. Its towers are reminiscent of La Giralda in Seville, Spain.

Every Friday, a most diverse audience gathers in front of the Palacio de los Capitanes Generales to listen to a band whose repertoire is as varied as they are (see Chapter 1).

Such is the space through which the life of the Centro Histórico flows. This is a space being revived through a constant effort at conservation that unites the old and the new, that joins complete respect for what is historically characteristic with creative acceptance of the contemporary, which in turn cannot but integrate the valuable legacy it carries within.

José Martí (1853–1895), patriot, freedom fighter, and poet, is Cuba's national hero.

Inscription on monument base: 24 DE FEBRERO DE 1895

7

SIGNS OF THE TIMES: HAVANA'S REPUBLICAN LANDMARKS REVISITED

Lillian Guerra

lanked by the colonial promenade known as El Prado and the raucous commercial district of Calzada de Monte (Monte Street), the architectural and political center of Havana reflects the historic aspirations of a passionately anti-imperialist nation as well as the neocolonial contradictions that undermined its existence for much of the twentieth century.

After three guerrilla wars to establish Cuban independence from Spain, a cross-class, racially diverse force of patriots emerged from the devastation of nearly thirty years of fighting to face the stillbirth of a dream: that dream was the nation that revolutionary leaders like Antonio Maceo and José Martí had once promised would be the first country of the Americas to transcend the accumulated inequalities and injustices of slavery. Shaped by multiple U.S. military occupations after 1898, the U.S.

Congress's imposition of the Platt Amendment in the 1901 Cuban Constitution ensured continued intervention (both diplomatic and military) in Cuba's political process whenever U.S. officials deemed it necessary. Thus, successively elected governments of the Cuban Republic found governing Cuba for the good of Cuba and the Cubans practically impossible. Thanks to unparalleled advantages granted during U.S. military occupations to foreign businesses, Cubans quickly witnessed the revival of sugar production based on the same exploitative rhythms of the past. Soon a large-scale, foreign-dominated plantation system anchored Cuba ever more deeply in the boom-and-bust cycles of a sugar monoculture. Subsidized mass importation of Spanish immigrants meant to "whiten" the country deepened the control that Spanish merchants had historically exercised over urban trade. By the mid-1910s, the combination

Holiday in Havana, Cuba.

You can see people carrying the Cuban and American flags and a big bass drum during the celebration depicted in this undated postcard.

of corruption and collaboration with U.S. officials who served as shadow advisors to Cuban presidents prompted the creation of a new fabulously wealthy elite. By the 1920s, that elite's legitimacy and power resided more in Washington than in the fields, factories, schoolrooms, or middle-class offices of republican Cuba. For this reason, protest and armed revolutionary activity meant to restore the egalitarian goals of Cuba's independence wars defined the first thirty years of the Cuban Republic (1902–33) just as much as neocolonialism and government repression did.

Confronted with political conditions that were often precarious at best, national administrations, especially those of José Miguel Gómez (1909–13), Mario Menocal (1914–22), and Gerardo Machado (1926–33), worked hard to provide citizens with evidence of Cuba's independence and a more promising future through the visible grandeur and massive (if temporary) employment programs of public works. Buildings, parks, and statuary thus reflected what most Cubans did not find in the struggles of their daily lives: national pride and symbols of a patriotic triumph over the tyranny of the past. Dwarfed by the mammoth luminosity of the Capitolio Nacional (National Capitol; see Chapter 8) and the grassy garden splendor of the Parque de la Fraternidad Americana (Park of Pan-American Fraternity), both built by President-turned-dictator Machado in the late 1920s, sumptuous relics and iconic places origi-

This postcard shows the celebration of the founding of the Republic of Cuba on May 20, 1902.

Inauguracion de la Republica Cubana y Subida de la bandera en el Morro.

The cigar box label (above) and the postcards reproduced on these two pages illustrate the attention given to Cuba's newly established independence and Cuban-American relations in the early years of the twentieth century. The postcard at top, opposite, pictures José Miguel Gómez and Alfredo Zayas, Liberal Party candidates for president and vice-president, who won the election in 1908 and were inaugurated in 1909.

FOR the Stars and Stripes and Cuba's cause
We honor the Boys in Blue;
They are near to us and dear to us,
And so is Old Glory too.

114 INAUGURACION PRESIDENCIAL CUBANA

Tobacco plantation. - Vega de tabaco.

REPUBLICA DE CUBA

The Parque de Colón (Columbus Park) contained exotic gardens and pathways. It was replaced by the Parque de la Fraternidad.

Avenida de Bolívar (Bolivar Avenue), commonly called Reina, leads toward Sagrado Corazón church.

PLAZA DE LA FRATERNIDAD, FRATERNITY PARK, HAVANA, CUBA

These images show opposite sides of the Parque de la Fraternidad. The postcard view was taken from the telephone company tower, which can be seen on the right in the recent photograph.

Habana, Parque Fraternidad y Avenida Bolivar

Fraternity Square and Bolivar Avenue

1 B-H608

The street commonly called Monte, which leads to the southwest, is officially named Máximo Gómez.

CUBAN TELEPHONE COMPANY, HAVANA,
ASSOCIATED WITH THE
INTERNATIONAL TELEPHONE & TELEGRAPH CORPORATION

nally crafted by the colonial era's slave-owning planters were removed, displaced, or simply revamped.

The earliest of these breaks with the past came with the re-creation of Havana's Parque Central (Central Park; see Chapter 8), a large, open-air plaza designed in the late Spanish colonial era to spiral out from a pedestal that supported the corpulent likeness of Queen Isabella II. With Spain's defeat at the hands of Cuban forces and U.S. troops in 1898, Cuban patriots moved quickly to topple the image of the queen. However, when pro-U.S. annexationist Cubans replaced Isabella's statue

The telephone company tower faces the northwestern side of Parque de la Fraternidad.

HOTEL SARATOGA
HAVANA, CUBA

The Saratoga Hotel, which faces the eastern side of the Parque de la Fraternidad, is twelve stories high, although it is designed so that it appears to have just five floors.

with a smaller version of the U.S. Statue of Liberty during the subsequent U.S. military occupation (1898–1902), a timely hurricane destroyed the hastily fashioned imitation on October 10, 1901, the very anniversary of Cuba's historic call for independence! (Few critics of the U.S. presence could resist the temptation to celebrate "divine" intervention on their behalf.) Afterward, an empty pedestal remained at the center of the park until 1905, when tens of thousands of Cubans joined General Máximo Gómez and other veteran leaders of the independence wars to unveil the giant, majestic statue of José Martí, Cuba's chief anti-imperialist ideologue. Martí's premature death at the start of the last and most radical independence war in May of 1895 inspired generations of Cubans to lament his passing as the first tragic turning point in Cuba's long-term struggle for liberation.

During the early Republic, another similarly recrafted and reimagined public space could be found near the monument to Martí in Parque Colón. Once built to honor America's original conquistador, Christopher Columbus, the park became the focal point of the Sixth Pan-American Conference of 1928. Attended by dignitaries from nearly every country of Latin America, the Pan-American Conference also marked the first and only visit to Cuba by a sitting U.S. president, Calvin Coolidge. However, the multiple occupations the U.S. military was carrying out at the time (in Haiti, Panama, and Nicaragua), and the widespread economic leverage that Washington's long-term reliance on "gunboat diplomacy" had achieved across the region, made it difficult to discern whether the conference celebrated hemispheric unity or Latin American

political elites' acceptance of U.S. control. For the emerging nationalist opposition in Cuba, there was little doubt: officials of the Machado administration who had meticulously orchestrated the park's redesign and inauguration highlighted their own hypocrisy by touting Latin American independence and related ideals. Renamed the Parque de la Fraternidad Americana, its grounds were punctuated by royal palms, symbols of the Cuban nation, and equally numerous busts of key Latin American independence leaders such as Simón Bolívar. Surrounded by men who, like him, claimed to be Bolívar's "heirs," President Machado presided over the planting of an enormous ceiba tree in the middle of the park. Earth brought from each one of the twenty-one participating republics filled the ominous wrought-iron gate surrounding the roots of the tree.

Perhaps most significantly, two opulent statues of the colonial era, both commissioned at the height of slavery in the late 1830s by the Conde de Villanueva, one of Havana's wealthiest slave owners, were refurbished by Machado's public works program in time for the Pan-American Conference. La India, a white Carrara marble fountain carved by Giuseppe Gaggini, now invited foreign guests and national observers to conceive her palm-leaf-clad body and fanciful feathered finery as newly symbolic. No longer did La India represent how Cuba's elite imagined the complicity of Cuba's indigenous inhabitants with their own imperial destruction: she now embodied the supposedly grateful willingness of the Western Hemisphere's indigenous populations as a whole to embrace European conquest and culture. Through the lens of Machado's

FRATERNITY TREE,
FRATERNITY PARK,
HAVANA, CUBA

The ceiba tree in Parque de
la Fraternidad was planted
in soil from many countries
of North and South America,
including the United States,
where the soil came from
Mount Vernon, the home of
George Washington.

dictatorship, La Fuente de La India became an icon of the triumph of his and other leaders' brand of exploitative modernity.

In like fashion, Gaggini's other great work, the Fuente de los Leones (Fountain of the Lions; see Chapter 3) was also made to invert the ideals of royalism it once embodied into evidence of the glories of the Cuban Republic and Machado's own efforts to expand Cuban prosperity through "mediated" democracy. Originally placed in the historic Plaza de San Francisco in Old Havana, the fountain now

stood before the monumental Capitolio, where, until the collapse of Machado's regime in the great social revolution of 1933, Cuban congressmen squandered national budgets and regularly failed to implement their own legislation favoring labor and other social rights.

In 1933, Cubans of all social classes backed a massive political upheaval and a revolutionary government that passed more progressive laws in its one hundred days of power than all previous republican administrations combined. After violently

Parque de la Fraternidad contains several sculpted busts of political leaders from the Americas. The Cubans honored Abraham Lincoln (1809–1865) with this portrait.

Benito Juárez (1806–1872) was president of Mexico between 1858 and 1872, a tumultuous time in Mexico's history when the French emperor Napoleon III attempted to take over the country, and Archduke Maximilian, an Austrian, served briefly as emperor of Mexico.

Simón Bolívar (1783–1830) was a general and forceful leader in the movement to liberate South American countries from Spanish domination.

41 - Estatua de la India (Plaza de la Fraternidad)   Statue of the „India" at Fraternity's Place.

The Fuente de La India sculpture looks past the Capitolio Nacional and the Parque Central toward El Paseo del Prado and the sea.

decapitating the Revolution of its brilliant leadership, U.S. mediators brought military strongman Fulgencio Batista and a series of puppet presidents to power. From 1934 to 1940, they presided over the bloody repression of revolutionary forces and striking workers. During this period and afterward, however, citizens reclaimed the magnificent public plazas, buildings, and icons of early republican Havana. Students defaced the images of Machado and U.S. Ambassador Sumner Welles on the massive bronze doors of the Capitolio. Protesters and baseball fanatics regularly congregated around the statue of José Martí in the Parque Central in impassioned debates over politics and sports. Perhaps most ironically of all, believers in the African-derived religion of Santería colonized the royal palms and ceiba tree of Machado's Parque de la Fraternidad, regularly leaving offerings to Changó, the great Yoruba deity of lightning. In short, however forced and self-serving political elites' architectural and political vision of early republican Cuba might have been, citizens' anti-imperialist identity not only survived to reassert itself, but it ultimately redefined public spaces to embody the diversity and democratic ideals that Cuba's independence wars and nationhood had represented all along. For this reason, Havana's republican landmarks today do not invoke tragedy or failure, but resistance, optimism, and that deeply Cuban tradition of longing for a brighter, freer political future.

The statue of La India, which holds the city's coat of arms and a cornucopia, is also known as Noble Havana.

CAPITOL BUILDING

The Capitolio, patterned on the Capitol in Washington, D.C., was built by the American firm Purdy & Henderson and inaugurated on May 20, 1929. One of the old picture postcards of it says: *The Capitol Building is a marvel of Engineering, Sculpture and Painting. Built at a cost of over sixteen million dollars it represents everything modern in construction and is considered the most beautiful palace in Latin America.*

The bust of Abraham Lincoln
is pictured with the Capitolio
in the background.

The Capitolio Nacional's neoclassical design is reminiscent of the U.S. Capitol building. However, its dome more closely resembles that of the Panthéon in Paris. Originally built as the seat of the Cuban congress, the Capitolio has been used since the 1960s by the Ministerio de Ciencia, Tecnología y Medio Ambiente (Ministry of Science, Technology and the Environment).

8

CAPITOLIO NACIONAL AND PARQUE CENTRAL

Mario Coyula

The massive Capitolio Nacional extends for two full blocks along the Prado from San José to Dragones streets. It was completed in 1929 after a harrowing process of design changes, construction freezes, and demolition of work already done. The participating architects included Eugenio Rayneri Sr. and Jr., Evelio Govantes and Félix Cabarrocas, and Raúl Otero and José María Bens Arrarte, among others. Especially interesting are the central dome that towers more than 300 feet (91 meters), the wide entrance stairway, and the impressive Salón de los Pasos Perdidos (Hall of Lost Steps). Two large statues by the Italian sculptor Angelo Zanelli flank the main steps, and on entering the building one encounters Zanelli's gilded bronze image of the Republic as well. More than 55 feet (17 meters) high, it was considered the second-largest such interior image in the world when it was installed.

The Capitolio's grounds were designed by the French landscape architect and urban planner Jean-Claude Nicolas Forestier, who also led the team that designed the neighboring Parque de la Fraternidad Americana (see Chapter 7).

The Parque Central, a beautiful tree-lined plaza across a busy intersection from the Capitolio Nacional, occupies the space created in 1877 by the joining of three small plazas outside one of the gates in the city's former wall. The defensive wall that surrounded La Habana Vieja took a long time to build (from 1674 to 1797), and by the time it was finished, the city's expansion had left it far behind. Thus, the new Parque Central, located just beyond the old Monserrate Gate, became a hinge linking La Habana Vieja to Centro Habana, the nineteenth century to the twentieth, and two different kinds of properties as well. One of the buildings facing the

El Trabajo (Work) and *La Virtud Tutelar* (The Tutelary Virtue) stand at the top of La Escalinata (the 55 steps leading to the main entrance of the Capitolio). The sculptures are 21 feet (6.5 meters) tall.

park, the Manzana de Gómez (Gómez Block), was constructed in two stages (1892 and 1917) to reflect the enclosed shopping galleries then in vogue in the large European cities. It features two diagonal internal corridors that cross in the middle of the building, and beveled corners on the outside where they end. This kind of commercial structure was itself a transition between the small European-style shops along the narrow streets of Obispo and O'Reilly in the old walled city, and the grand U.S.-style department stores along Galiano, San Rafael, and Neptuno in the new shopping district of Centro Habana.

The park features a statue of Cuba's national hero José Martí by José Vilalta de Saavedra, the

The Salón de los Pasos Perdidos (Hall of Lost Steps), named for its acoustic properties, has a coffered ceiling, ornamented windows, and inlaid marble floors. Simple benches and gilded lamps are the only furnishings.

La Estatua de la República (Statue of the Republic), covered with gold leaf, dominates the main hall of the Capitolio. The central design on the inlaid marble floor marks Kilometer Zero, from which all distances in Cuba are measured.

The Capitolio's symmetrical landscape design consists of paved walkways interspersed with grassy areas highlighted by royal palms and decorative lights on thick columns.

The pedestal in Parque Central was empty for a period of time after independence and before the erection of the statue of José Martí. The most notable change, however, is the presence of shade trees; formerly the park was largely open to the sun's rays.

In these two undated postcards, the Manzana de Gómez (Gómez Block) is pictured before and after it was remodeled in 1917.

HABANA. Parque, Hotel Plaza y Politeama. Plaza Hotel & Polyteama Building.

Habana: Parque Central, Manzana Gomez, Hotel Plaza.
Central Park, Gomez Building, Plaza Hotel.

The appearance of the Manzana de Gómez has changed very little since the postcard image at the bottom of the opposite page was made. One of the interior corridors faces Plaza de Albear.

José Martí's statue is decorated by dignitaries on the anniversary of his birth, January 28, 1853. On this day, school children parade around the perimeter of Parque Central in various costumes while official ceremonies take place at the sculpture. In the recent photograph, adolescents in secondary school uniforms stand near the monument.

STATUE OF GENERAL MARTI, CENTRAL PARK, Havana, Cuba
10. PUBL. BY DIAMOND NEWS CO. HAVANA

most important Cuban sculptor of his time. In 1960, architect Eugenio Batista redesigned the Parque Central, bringing it to its current form. Always alive with pedestrians and visitors, the park is home to the Hot Corner, a daily gathering of baseball fans who are generally arguing at the top of their lungs.

The demolition of the old wall freed up space not only for the park, but also for building on a wide strip of terrain that had been kept empty for military reasons. This strip, stretching from Calzada de Monte at its southern end, past the Parque de la Fraternidad Americana, to La Punta fortress at the water's edge, became home to a number of important buildings that gave Havana a newly monumental tone. By the end of the 1920s, Buenos Aires and Havana had become the two great cities of Latin America.

Facing the Parque Central itself on the west side is the Hotel Inglaterra, whose current appearance dates from 1915, surrounding a core first built in 1856 and then remodeled in 1891. The original neoclassical design took on new eclectic elements, especially

The Esquina Caliente (Hot Corner) got its name from Cuban slang for third base. Here, men's passions run high as they discuss béisbol (baseball) under the shade trees of Parque Central.

The Hotel Telégrafo, Acera del Louvre, and Hotel Inglaterra stretch southward toward the Centro Gallego and Capitolio in this photograph. Their open terraces provide shade during the sunny hours, and food and drink at almost any hour.

Visitors at the Hotel Inglaterra (HAVANA, Cuba) watching the crowd from the Balconies on Independence day May the 20th.

A floor was added to the Hotel Inglaterra between the time the postcard image and the recent photograph were made. The hotel, which contains 83 guest rooms, boasts that it was "one of the first hotels built with American capital."

The dining room of the Hotel Inglaterra is decorated with stained-glass windows, colorful mosaic tile panels, and relief sculpture on the ceiling and columns.

The high ceilings and supporting arches of the Hotel Telégrafo are remnants of the earlier building on the site.

PLAZA HOTEL — HAVANA, CUBA   6A-H1870

Before becoming a hotel, the Pedroso family mansion was head office for the newspaper *El Diario de la Marina* during the tumultuous years of the Cuban struggle for independence. During the 1950s, the hotel operated a popular casino.

N.º 28 HABANA TEATRO NACIONAL Y HOTEL DE INGLATERRA.—NATIONAL THEATRE & INGLATERRA HOTEL

In this series of images, an early postcard shows the small Teatro Tacón, which was later encompassed in the Centro Gallego. A model displayed inside the theater illustrates how the Centro Gallego was built around the old theater.

the Sevillian-style patio. Beneath the shaded porticos of this building and the nearby Hotel Telégrafo, also of nineteenth-century origin, extended the famous Acera del Louvre (Louvre sidewalk), home to a café of the same name. The Acera del Louvre was the habitual gathering place of many young Cuban men who met to conspire against Spain and later fought in the Independence War of 1895. Restored in 1982, the Inglaterra has been declared a national landmark. The Hotel Telégrafo, which was rebuilt and reopened in 2001, retains some arches from the original building, and the Acera del Louvre is still intact. Opposite a corner on the other side of the park, meanwhile, the architect José Mata designed the Hotel Plaza, constructed in 1908, by remodeling and enlarging the old mansion of the Pedroso family. This building was remodeled again in 1991.

Also facing the park, just to the south of the

Ball Room, Centro Gallego, Habana, Cuba — Salón de Baile, Centro Gallego

CENTRO GALLEGO, HAVANA, CUBA

The back of a similar postcard depicting the Centro Gallego reads: *This nice building belongs to Gallego's Association of about 50,000 people, who like the Asturians, Dependientes, Clerks, Castillians, Canarians, etc, pay the sum of $2.00 monthly and get all benefits of the Club House and Sanatorium. The theater is modern and comfortable, in the European style, entertaining the best shows of Comedy, Drama, Reviews, Opera, Concerts, Movies, etc.*

The Centro Gallego today houses a post office, an art gallery, and the Gran Teatro de la Habana, home of the Ballet Nacional de Cuba, founded in 1948 by Alicia Alonso, and the Cuban National Opera. Ballet and opera are performed in the Teatro García Lorca; two smaller halls host concerts. Upcoming events are posted under the colonnades on the sidewalk.

Mario Coyula   155

HAVANA: CENTRAL PARK, ASTURIAN CLUB

122623-N

The Centro Asturiano palace is now a fine-arts museum showing paintings and sculptures by non-Cuban artists.

Inglaterra, one of the major regional societies of Spanish immigrants built the Centro Gallego (Galician Center) in 1915, designed by the Belgian architect Paul Belau, who five years later would also design the Palacio Presidencial along with Carlos Maruri. The Centro Gallego was a palace that surrounded (and maintained intact) the venerable Teatro Tacón (1838). Among the many notable events that took place in this theater was the Italian Antonio Meucci's invention between 1849 and 1850 of the telephone, which he called a "talking telegraph." Outside, the Centro Gallego is distinguished by the profuse decoration of its typically eclectic façades. Inside, the visitor is struck by a magnificent central staircase with skylight illumination.

In 1927, another important society of Spanish immigrants, in this case Asturians, built its own palace, the Centro Asturiano, following a contest-winning plan by the Spanish architect Manuel del Busto. Like the Centro Gallego, the Capitolio, and almost all the major new buildings of Havana in the first third of the twentieth century, it was constructed by the contractor Purdy & Henderson. With its impressive central staircase crowned by a splendid stained-glass skylight, the Centro Asturiano evidently sought to surpass that of its Galician rivals.

Across from the park on the southern side stands the Teatro Payret. The Payret's current appearance dates from the 1940 total remodeling of the old 1877 theater of the same name—a five-story building with a cast-iron roof crafted in Brussels.

Also facing the Parque Central, but on the north side, is the Hotel Parque Central, built in 1998 in the square block surrounded by the Prado, Neptuno, Zulueta, and Virtudes. The designers of this new hotel incorporated a surviving fragment of traditional colonnaded arcade remaining from the colonial buildings that had occupied the site.

The Parque Central serves as the crown of the Paseo del Prado.

Habana: Prado, Neptuno y Hotel Plaza.
Prado, Central Park and Plaza Hotel.

The Hotel Parque Central, one of the most luxurious in Havana, features 277 guest rooms organized around an interior courtyard, several restaurants and bars, and a rooftop swimming pool.

9

PASEO DEL PRADO

Leland Cott

The Paseo del Prado is one of the most beautiful streets in the world. It is certainly without equal in Havana. It was originally constructed in 1772, under the rule of the Spanish governor, the Marqués de la Torre, as one of Havana's first promenades outside of the city walls. Its current design is the result of a 1929 restoration and redesign of the original street, the Alameda de Isabel II, by the French landscape architect Jean-Claude Nicolas Forestier and the important Cuban architect Raúl Otero. Prior to 1929, the Paseo del Prado was also known as Calle Ancha and then later as Paseo de Martí. Whatever its name during previous incarnations, it is now simply known to everyone in Havana, resident or visitor, as "El Prado."

The Paseo del Prado is available to all residents of Havana and supports a wide variety of activities along its eight-block length. At any given time, one can see lovers strolling and sitting, young children at recess playing their schoolyard games, intricate roller-blading contests and, of course, baseball. Here, artists exhibit their paintings on weekends as people also gather to exchange apartments. It is the quintessential urban street—one that we architects and urban designers dream of creating—supporting active pedestrian street life, automobile traffic, public transportation, and generous amounts of shade from its rich canopy of ficus trees. The Paseo del Prado connects the heart of Centro Habana at the Capitol building and the Parque Central with the eastern end of the Malecón, Havana's iconic waterfront boulevard. Serving as a linear extension of the Parque Central, its design visually links the dome of the Capitol with the lighthouse of Morro Castle at the mouth of Havana harbor.

Until recently, the Paseo del Prado was in a state

161

8263. PRADO, LOOKING NORTH, HAVANA, CUBA. COPYRIGHT, 1904, BY DETROIT PHOTOGRAPHIC CO.

Regale su vista contemplando el Prado, y reciba recuerdos de su amiga María Prado

The changes in the Prado after its redesign in 1929 are easily seen in these two images. A street-level walkway exposed to the sun and illuminated by gaslight was converted into an elevated concourse shaded by a canopy of ficus trees and lighted at night by decorative streetlamps.

Paséo del Prado was the city's most elegant street when it was developed. By the 1950s, many prominent families were abandoning their mansions here to move to the more modern neighborhoods to the west.

Four pairs of life-sized lion sculptures are a prominent feature on the Paseo del Prado. They were modeled after a bronze lion brought to Havana from England and cast in the studios of Darden Beller.

The Cuban poet Juan Clemente Zenea (1832–1871) was killed by Spanish troops for supporting the movement for Cuban independence. The scaffolding on the left side of the photograph supports the façade of the former Packard Hotel, which is slated to be rebuilt by Spanish architect Rafael Moneo.

of semi-ruin, but now, thanks to recent intervention from the Office of the City Historian, this elegant pedestrian promenade is slowly being restored to its former state of beauty and grace.

A pair of large bronze lions stands proudly at the Prado's southern entrance opposite Parque Central at Calle Neptuno. Two additional pairs of bronze lions flank the intersection of Calle Colón as it crosses the Prado and another pair faces the sea at Calle San Lázaro. Near the Malecón is a sculpture of a seated figure, the poet and martyr J. C. Zenea. Benches and low walls, made of familiar Havana coral rock, line the pedestrian portion of the promenade for its entire length. This street furniture provides a massive base for the decorated bronze lampposts, each of which supports an elaborate array of large lanterns. This long (2,133 feet; 650 meters) urban room is as beautiful as ever, and with its unique pedestrian scale, this tree-lined shady promenade is *the* place to be on a hot day.

The number of lanterns on each lamppost depends on its location. The five-armed lampposts are near Calle Neptuno and the Malecón and at the intersection of Calle Colón. Those with three lanterns line the steps leading from the pedestrian walkway to the street level; the balance are two-armed lampposts.

Habana: Paseo del Prado ó de Martí. Residences at Prado Promenade.

The Pedro Estevez house is the home today of the Escuela Primaría Especial (Special Primary School) Emma Rosa Chuy.

As you would expect, there are a number of fine buildings along the Paseo del Prado. Among them is the Pedro Estevez house of 1905 designed by the French architect Charles Brun. This residence was eventually purchased by the first U.S. consul to Cuba and is notable as one of the earliest buildings in Cuba built of reinforced concrete. President José Miguel Gómez constructed his residence in 1915.

The ground-level portico was originally enclosed by metal balustrades but was later opened to be used as public space, thus complying with regulations governing public and private space along the Paseo del Prado. Also of note along the Prado is the Casino Español, built in 1914 by a Spanish immigrant association as a community meeting place. Of a different era and style is the Teatro Fausto, designed in 1938

Built as the residence of José Miguel Gómez, Cuba's second president, this house has been converted into a hotel that advertises its "grandiose marble stairway and . . . tile-and-mahogany-lined dining room."

Habana: Casino Español.
Spanish Club.

The former Casino Español (Spanish Club) is now the location of the Palacio de Los Matrimonios de La Habana Vieja (Marriage Licensing Bureau).

The Art Deco–style Teatro Fausto, which seats nearly 1,700, was built with sound-blocking walls to protect theatergoers from outside noise. Originally a movie theater, it has become a venue for live comedy shows.

by Saturnino Parajón. Interestingly, this streamlined building is as much a part of its context as are the previous three structures, partly due to its compatible height and the alignment of its first-floor covered colonnades on both elevations. It is evident that the original design requirement of a continuous covered street façade along the Paseo del Prado gives the street a degree of visual harmony while also providing much needed shade for pedestrian activity. Finally, the Hotel Sevilla Biltmore with its distinctive ten-story tower, designed by the American firm Schultze and Weaver, provides wonderful views up and down the Prado from its top floor banquet and dance hall.

HABANA. Prado y San Lázaro
Prado and St. Lázaro Street.

This Art Nouveau building, which houses a café, has been dwarfed by more recent nearby construction. Street life also changed as public streetcars on calle San Lázaro have been replaced by private motorcycles and cars.

Habana: Paseo de Martí o Prado-Centro Dependientes.
Martí or Prado Promenade-Clerk Association Building

The Centro de Dependientes del Comercio (Commercial Employees' Center), a Venetian Gothic–style building by architect Arturo Amigó, was constructed in 1907. Its owners were members of an organization of commercial tradesmen. This contrasted with owners of buildings such as the Casino Español and the American Club on the Prado, and the Centro Asturiano and Centro Gallego on Parque Central, who shared cultural roots.

The small sculptures of dancers facing the stairway of the Centro de Dependientes del Comercio allude to its present use as a school of classical ballet. One of the pleasures of walking along the Paseo del Prado is hearing classical music wafting from the building's open windows.

HABANA: LA PUNTA, MALECON Y AVENIDA MACEO DESDE EL MAR.

LA PUNTA FORT, MALECON AND MACEO AVENUE FROM THE OUTSIDE.   106639

This undated postcard view of the Prado was made before construction of the Hotel Sevilla tower, which was completed in 1928, and the Capitolio, completed in 1929.

There is a great deal to be learned from this street as Havana looks for new models of urban design to cope with increased tourism and development. Forestier's inspired design lifts the central pedestrian spine about three feet above the two lanes of traffic on each side, similar to the Ramblas in Barcelona, thus elevating this eight-block-long linear plaza above the noisier, less pedestrian-friendly activities along its edges. The smooth terrazzo paving under foot provides a welcome relief from the broken pavement that typifies a good deal of Havana today. Where the cross streets intersect the pedestrian promenade, granite steps bring the pedestrian to the grade below. The Paseo del Prado is an urban oasis without equal.

P. & O. TWIN SCREW PASSENGER STEAMSHIP "CUBA"

341 FT. LONG, 47 FT. WIDE, SPEED 17 KNOTS PER HOUR, PASSENGER CAPACITY 512   5A-H555

Of the many changes in these views of the Prado made from Morro Castle, the most notable are the appearance of tall buildings such as apartments and the pink Hotel Sevilla tower. The large building east of Paseo del Prado (on the left in the postcard images) is the so-called new jail, which was demolished in 1938. The remains of the Packard Hotel, also along the east side of the Prado, are visible in the recent photograph. The unsightly wall on the right appeared when the building on the corner of Prado and the Malecón was demolished recently; a new building is being constructed in this location.

Leland Cott   175

10

MALECÓN

Mario Coyula

Havana's relation to the sea is essential to the city's history and its image. The Cuban capital's sheltered harbor brought both riches and power, yet for a long time the city feared to approach the coastline, because the shore was seen as a source of danger. By 1860, the brilliant Cuban engineer Francisco de Albear was proposing the construction of a *malecón*, or seawall and promenade, which would also form a part of Havana's defense system, but this project was never carried out. Through the rest of the nineteenth century, the water's edge remained visually uninspiring, a place where garbage was dumped and sewer ditches ended, ironically coexisting with some ugly wooden structures that served as bathhouses, since the health benefits of sea baths had recently been recognized. On May 6, 1901, under the first U.S. intervention government of Cuba (1898–1902), construction of the Malecón

of Havana began where the Paseo del Prado met the coast, alongside the Hotel Miramar. This new seaside drive began in the shadow of the old Castillo de la Punta fortress, designed by Bautista Antonelli and Cristóbal de Roda and constructed over the period from 1589 to about 1600.

The first stretch of the Malecón reached Calle Crespo, 1,640 feet (500 meters) to the west, in 1902. Its dominant landmark was the Union Club, a structure with an attractive façade of coral-formed stone and a characteristic loggia adorned with pillars featuring sculptures of human heads atop inverted pyramid shapes. The preexisting buildings, originally fronting on Calle San Lázaro a block inland with their backs turned to the sea, now required the addition of new façades facing the promenade, with high, colonnaded porticos for pedestrians to use. This passageway ran continuously from building to

At the foot of the Paseo del Prado, where the land meets the sea, is a point of land called La Punta. Owing to its position at the harbor entrance, it was developed as a military stronghold. In peaceful times, however, it served as a popular gathering place for events such as band concerts, carnival celebrations, and hailing the arrival and departure of ships. The fortress is now a national monument housing a museum of maritime and underwater archaeology, the Museo de San Salvador de La Punta.

La Punta, Havana, Cuba.

building, because the old system of narrow buildings with shared side walls remained in force.

In 1909, the Malecón reached the major north-south axis of the Calzada de Belascoaín, where the Vista Alegre bar stood. There it paused, while its builders faced the obstacle of San Lázaro Cove and the adjoining La Reina gun battery, part of the city's coastal defense. By 1916, the cove had been filled and the Malecón extended to the old San Lázaro tower, but three years later a hurricane ripped up the land-fill, which had to be rebuilt. In 1921 the seaside drive reached Calle 23, previously the Calzada de Medina. This involved filling several old quarries and then the Tanganana Cave, which brought the Malecón

to the broad esplanade where in 1925 a monument was erected to the victims of the 1898 explosion of the battleship U.S.S. *Maine* in Havana Harbor. The sinking of the *Maine* had sparked U.S. intervention in Cuba's war for independence from Spain. The monument, a work of the important Cuban artist and architect Félix Cabarrocas, matched the foot-print of the battleship and incorporated two of its large cannons. When the devastating hurricane of 1926 totally destroyed the monument, it was imme-diately reconstructed. The two tall columns of its central motif were crowned by an American eagle, taken down after the triumph of the Cuban Revo-lution in 1959 to be replaced by a dove offered by

6001. Memorial Wall to the Cuban Students,
Havana, Cuba.

Memorial a los Estudiantes de Medicina (Medical Students' Memorial), near the intersection of Paseo del Prado and the Malecón, honors eight Cuban medical students, aged sixteen to nineteen, who were shot by Spanish colonial authorities on November 27, 1871. This fragment of the wall in front of which the attack took place is preserved in their memory and the anniversary of the event is still honored.

The former Union Club was built by a group of English businessmen during the so-called Fat Cows period between the two world wars. The building has been beautifully restored. Architectural details include a curved marble staircase leading from ground level to the floor above, where a balcony adorned with herms overlooks the sea. The building now houses the Centro Hispano-Americano de Cultura (Spanish-American Cultural Center), a museum that contains a theater, a computer room, a library, and two large spaces used for temporary art exhibitions.

U.S.S. *Maine*, a steel warship with a crew of 354 men, exploded in Havana harbor on February 15, 1898, killing more than 250 seamen. Thought at the time to be an act of aggression, the incident precipitated the United States's declaration of war against Spain on April 25, 1898. It has been verified recently that the explosion was, in fact, caused by heat from the ship's boilers, which were located too close to the ammunition storage area. The base of this monument, laid out to mimic the dimensions of the U.S.S. *Maine*, incorporates cannons and chains salvaged from the battleship.

U. S. S. "MAINE" MONUMENT,
HAVANA, CUBA

The inscription reads: That the people of the Island of Cuba are, and of right ought to be, free and independent. —Joint resolution of the Congress of the United States of America on December 19, 1898.

The inscription added in 1961 reads: To the victims of the Maine who were sacrificed to the hunger of the imperialists in their eagerness to seize the island of Cuba.

The site of the former music pavilion, at the intersection of the Paseo del Prado and the Malecón, has become one of Havana's busiest traffic intersections.

Pablo Picasso, but the promised peace symbol never arrived. Meanwhile, that same hurricane year of 1926 brought the demolition, in this case by human hands, of the bandstand at the intersection of the Malecón and the Prado where the Municipal Band used to play. This demolition was required to link the Malecón with the Avenida del Puerto, a tree-lined boulevard designed in 1928 like the Prado, by Jean-Claude Nicolas Forestier, which straightened

the western side of the harbor entrance as far as the Castillo de La Real Fuerza in the Plaza de Armas.

To build the next westward stretch of the Malecón, from the *Maine* monument to Calle G along the shore of El Vedado, involved rounding the rocky promontory holding the Baterí Santa Clara and reclaiming a large area from the sea. Atop that same promontory the well-known U.S. architects McKim, Mead & White designed the Hotel

184 MALECÓN

HOTEL NACIONAL DE CUBA

The eclectic architecture of the Hotel Nacional includes Moorish-Spanish, Art Deco, neoclassical, and neocolonial designs. A large garden overlooking the sea contains an enormous cannon from the battery of Santa Clara, formerly located on the site.

Nacional, whose construction began in 1928. Now designated a national monument, the hotel bears a strong resemblance to the Breakers in Palm Beach. Beyond the hotel site, the Malecón's builders had to eliminate two more gun batteries—Number 3 (opposite where the 1950s U.S. Embassy and current U.S. Interests Section would be built) and Number 4 (where the Parque Martí sports facility stands). The Malecón finally reached Calle G in 1930, the same year the Hotel Nacional opened its doors.

Several monuments to heroes of the independence wars appear along the length of the seaside drive. Near the beginning, in line with the Palacio Presidencial (now Museo de la Revolución), is the bronze statue of Generalísimo Máximo Gómez by the Italian sculptor Aldo Gamba, who won the commission in a contest in 1916 but had to wait twenty years for the statue's inauguration. Between Belascoaín and Marina, where the San Lázaro Cove was filled, stands another bronze monument, this one to Lieutenant General Antonio Maceo, who died in combat in 1896. Italian sculptor Domenico Boni won this contest in 1911, and the complex of figures was inaugurated five years later and forms a part of the Parque Maceo. At the intersection of Malecón and G, U.S. designers Felix de Weldon and Elbert

The U.S. Interests Section, a part of the Swiss embassy, represents the United States in Cuba. The black flags and poles were installed by the Cuban government to obscure messages broadcast from an electronic billboard on the building.

HABANA. PALACIO PRESIDENCIAL

PRESIDENT'S HOUSE   123537

The Presidential Palace, designed by the Cuban architect Carlos Maruri and the Belgian architect Paul Belau, was the official residence of the presidents of the Cuban Republic from 1920 to 1960. It currently houses the Museo de la Revolución (Museum of the Revolution).

MÁXIMO GOMEZ MONUMENT

Generalísimo Máximo Gómez (1836–1905) was military commander in Cuba's War of Independence (1895–98), the last three months of which are known in the United States as the Spanish-American War. The neo-Rococo building in the background was the residence of Dionisio Velasco, constructed between 1912 and 1914 by the Cuban architect Francisco Ramírez Ovando and the Venezuelan builder Paulino Naranjo. The building, Velasco Palace, presently serves as the Embassy of Spain.

Habana: Parque y Monumento a Maceo
Maceo Park and Monument

122632

Maceo Park is located near the former bullring on Belascoaín Street and the jai alai fronton facility. The 25-story Hermanos Ameijeiras Hospital, built in a modern style between 1958 and 1980, sits behind the park and overlooks the sea.

Lieutenant General Antonio Maceo (1845–1896), the son of a Venezuelan mulatto and a free Cuban black woman, is a hero of the wars that ended Spanish domination over Cuba.

Peets created a bronze and black granite monument to Major General Calixto García, hero of the three independence wars who, as José Martí said, wore his general's star on his forehead. Martí was alluding to the scar from the shot with which García tried to commit suicide rather than fall prisoner to the enemy. Begun in 1957, the monument was inaugurated on August 4, 1959.

When the Malecón was extended farther along the coast of El Vedado, from Calle G westward to the next large north-south boulevard, Paseo, a number of old bathing pools were destroyed. These had been dug out of the coastal coral beginning in 1864: El Progreso, facing the bottom of Calle E; Las Playas, facing D; Carneado, facing Paseo; as well as El Encanto, Las Delicias, and El Océano. Older residents of Vedado referred to Calle E as "Baños" because of El Progreso. At Paseo, the Malecón halted until the 1950s, blocked

Major General Calixto García (1839–1898) was a military leader in the Ten Years War (1868–78), the Cuban revolution, and the Spanish-American War. The essay *A Message to Garcia* by Elbert Hubbard, about a soldier who accomplishes a daunting mission, made García's name well known in the United States.

Santa Dorotea de Luna de la Chorrera Fortress was built to protect the mouth of the Almendares River, which was navigable at the time. Comprising storehouses, barracks for fifty men, and a drawbridge, it was severely damaged by the British in 1762.

by the nearly new Palacio de los Deportes. Besides national and international athletic competitions, the sports palace hosted visiting acts ranging from the ice-skating champion Sonja Henie to the Ringling Bros. and Barnum & Bailey Circus. In the mid-fifties, though, the Palacio, too, was razed to allow the completion of the Malecón. In 1979, part of its place was taken by a fountain, the Fuente de la Juventud, following a prize-winning design by Rómulo Fernández, José Cuendias, and others.

In 1958, the drive was completed to its conclusion at the small fortress called La Chorrera (built around 1645) that had guarded the entrance to the Río Almendares from pirates and privateers. The name Vedado (which means "prohibited") came, in fact, from a ban dating back to 1565, inspired by the fear of such landings. When this final stretch of the Malecón was built, the Vedado Tennis Club demanded a waterway under the road for passage of its rowing craft. The handsome mansion of this elegant club, whose members were nicknamed "marqueses," was remodeled in 1920 by the architects Rafecas & Tonarely. It is one of a number of buildings that still turn their backs on the Malecón because their builders did not foresee that the road would reach so far.

The Malecón presents great visual coherence in its first fourteen blocks, the ones forming the seaside edge of Centro Habana. That unity is reinforced by the narrow lots and shared walls of the buildings, the short blocks separated by narrow streets, the similar age and architecture of the buildings, and their unification by the high-roofed pedestrian porticos. The section that borders El Vedado presents a much more diluted image when viewed at close range, because construction in Vedado took longer to reach the shore, with a more amorphous result.

The Malecón today is well defined at its two ends by the colonial forts—La Punta to the east, along the neck of the bay with the iconic silhouette of the Morro visible immediately behind, and La Chorrera to the west at the river mouth. The two tunnels (under the bay and the river) also function visually as mouths or doors. The roadway and adjoining sidewalk form a cross-section of the historical evolution of Havana over 4 miles (nearly 7 kilometers) in length and stretching through four centuries of time, from La Habana Vieja past Centro Habana to El Vedado. The low seawall cannot contain the waves during tropical hurricanes or even some stormy days during the winter months, but the rest of the time it serves as an enormous bench on which thousands of Havana's residents convene in search of a refreshing sea breeze. The S-curve shape means that any point offers a view of both sea and city. The Malecón forms part of the characteristic image that Havana projects. In fact, it is the *face* of the city, its façade, or—better put—its front porch adjoining the sea. But there is a penalty to pay for this: during periodic floods the sea reclaims what was once partly its own. Flood or no flood, the constant salt spray corrodes everything except the stone that the sea covered, which is now lamentably scarce. Spray and floods also inhibit the growth of vegetation, whose shade is so essential given the climate. The construction of underwater barriers to dissipate the energy of the waves before they can break against the wall has been discussed, but it involves very costly investments.

The Malecón ends at the Río Almendares

MACEO OR GULF AVENUE

Although crossing the
Malecón from the city to
the sea can be treacherous
because of fast-moving
traffic, the seawall is a
favorite spot for enjoying the
sea breeze on a hot day.

196   MALECÓN

because privatization of the whole coastline beyond the river's mouth in the 1920s had blocked any possibility of its extension farther west. A 1950s proposal for a bridge to unite El Vedado's Primera Avenida (First Avenue) with that of Miramar on the other side was rejected. Instead came a tunnel, inaugurated in 1958, that replaced the so-called Puente de Pote (Pote's Bridge) which linked Vedado's Calzada with Quinta Avenida (Fifth Avenue) in Miramar. In 1959, the Malecón was linked to this tunnel by an entrance across from La Chorrera. The same speculative impulse—unleashed by the passage of the Horizontal Property Law of 1952—motivated construction of the series of condominium towers with water views at the other end of the Vedado section of the Malecón. An example is the Someillán Building, opposite the monument to the *Maine*, each of whose thirty stories was dedicated to a single luxury apartment. Within a few years, this boom threatened to raise a nearly continuous wall of tall buildings that would have blocked all views of the sea from the city itself, as well as the entrance of the breezes that cool and clean the air that residents of the capital breathe. Because the Malecón still forms one of the few routes for rapid east-west travel by car, pedestrians have a hard time crossing it. This limits the access of several hundred thousand people to the water's edge. If the Malecón has many problems, however, it also offers many opportunities. The large investments needed for rehabilitation of the infrastructure and conservation of the buildings could be financed in great part by the income that would result from these improvements.

On the left is the FOCSA building, designed by Ernesto Gómez Sampera and completed in 1956. Its 39 stories contain 373 apartments, a swimming pool, office space, a television studio, and a shopping center. Nearly 400 feet (121 meters) tall, its construction launched the era of tall buildings in Havana. The Someillán tower, on the right, was constructed in 1957 of reinforced concrete. Designed by architect Max Borges Recío, it is actually a complex of three multistory buildings facing the Malecón and the sea beyond. The U.S.S. *Maine* memorial appears in the foreground.

THE MORRO CASTLE IN A NORTH DAY.

On stormy days, windswept
sea spray covers the
sidewalks and street, forcing
closure of the Malecón.

198   MALECÓN

Generations of Cubans have fished along the Malecón, as these young men are doing on a windy November afternoon.

11

EL VEDADO

Pedro Contreras

To Habaneros from the late nineteenth century on, the words "El Vedado" signaled a special quality of life: the style offered by the magnificent neighborhood of this name on the western edge of the City of Havana, a style linked to the high economic and social rank of those who lived there. Earlier, however, "El Vedado" (literally, the barred or forbidden) signaled a prohibition against most access to this wooded area, imposed for reasons of military security. To prevent possible attacks by pirates or privateers, La Chorrera fortress was erected alongside the mouth of the Almendares River at the far western end of the area, and cannon batteries were mounted at several points along the rocky coast.

By 1859 there were already some small settlements of fishermen and quarry workers in Vedado, but in that year José Domingo Trigo, leader of a group promoting the rational urban development of the area, won approval for the street design and building regulations drawn up by the engineer Luis Yboleón Bosque. These plans were in tune with the most advanced ideas of the time, comparable to those employed in the expansion of Barcelona. Even today, the plans are admired for their positive use of the natural contours of the coast, wise adaptation to the natural landscape (something like a giant amphitheater from which to gaze at the sea), and the priority conceded to vegetation and the healthy sea breeze.

Construction began in El Carmelo at the far western end of Vedado and gradually moved eastward to join the preexisting Havana. The design featured square blocks 328 feet (100 meters) on a side, divided into rectangular lots whose narrow ends faced the street, with larger, square lots on the corners. At least 3 feet (1 meter) of open space was required between buildings, which had to be set off from the

HABANA. RESIDENCIA DEL DR. CÉSPEDES

DR. CESPEDES RESIDENCE

123543

The former residence of Dr. Carlos Miguel de Céspedes, now the "1830" restaurant, was built on a most privileged site, formerly occupied by fishermen's shacks, between the Castillo de la Chorrera fortress and the mouth of the Almendares River. Dr. Céspedes's beautiful neocolonial chalet enriched the setting with its large, exotic gardens featuring a Moorish-style gazebo alongside artistically arranged rock fragments and Japanese elements.

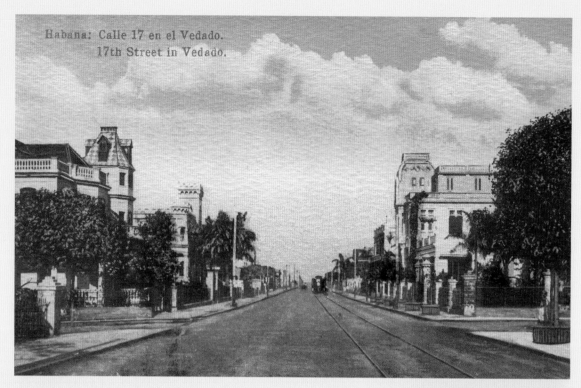

Habana: Calle 17 en el Vedado.
17th Street in Vedado.

Calle 17 was once known as "Millionaires' Street" thanks to the presence of the homes of some of the country's most important landlords and bankers. Today, some of those former residences house state institutions such as the Cuban Institute of Friendship among the Peoples (ICAP) and the National Union of Cuban Writers and Artists (UNEAC).

Habana: Vedado Tennis Club.

The Vedado Tennis Club (so-named, in English) was built in 1912 by Morales and Mata and expanded in 1920 with the addition of magnificent new function rooms. It was the club of choice for Vedado's "best families." Despite the name, it offered facilities for other sports in addition to tennis, such as baseball and rowing. After the Revolution, this club like many others was converted into a Workers' Social Club and opened free of charge to the public.

Pedro Contreras   205

Habana: Residencias en el Vedado, Calle O.
           Residences at Vedado, O. Street.

The stretch of Calle O shown in these views is that facing the monument to the victims of the explosion of the U.S.S. *Maine*. At the intersection of Calles O and 19 stands the picturesque former residence of the Martínez Piloto family, built at the turn of the twentieth century, which displays the historicist trend that began in that period of Cuban architecture. Today this "castle," painted in an unfortunate fashion, houses many families.

G 12041 A Cuban Home - Un Hogar Cubano, Habana.

Building homes in a Victorian-influenced vernacular style was a common practice in Vedado around 1900. The style came by way of the United States, and in Cuba it acquired new elements such as tall windows with jalousie shutters in the French style and ornamental curving iron grates. Very few such buildings can still be found, and those remaining are in ruinous condition.

street by front yards at least 16 feet (5 meters) deep, in addition to sidewalks and tree-planted beds along the curbs. A ban on buildings more than two stories high—which was respected for many years—gave the neighborhood a homogeneous character in spite of the great variety of architectural styles adopted. Another characteristic feature was the distribution throughout the neighborhood of entire square blocks left unbuilt, set aside for tree-shaded parks with benches and central gazebos or fountains.

Two grand avenues run parallel to the sea from east to west. One, despite having had various names in different historical periods, is universally referred to as Línea (line) because it was the original route of the railroad line running from Havana to the area of La Chorrera. The other, farther up the slope, is Calle 23. Over time, alongside the residences that line these avenues, have risen Neo-Gothic churches, excellent movie houses, and businesses of many sorts, including such restaurants as El Jardín, El Carmelo, and Las Delicias de Medina, all three surrounded by comfortable outdoor terraces shaded by colored awnings. Two more broad avenues, Calle G, or Avenida de los Presidentes (Avenue of the Presidents), and Paseo rise perpendicularly to Línea and Calle 23 and run uphill toward the height of land that holds the University of Havana campus, several large hospitals (toward the southeast), and

G 12053 New Havana, La Habana moderna.
G. City. Cuba. All quiet here so far. Yours. A. E. P. —

Calle Línea is one of the widest and best-known streets of Vedado. Since it was first laid out, Línea has provided the chief access to Vedado from Havana proper. Along its length, especially at its intersection with Calle B, buildings that date from the 1880s can be seen. Stylistically, these are related to the neoclassical villas of Cerro, another former suburb of the old city.

the Cementerio de Colón (toward the southwest). These two boulevards are the widest of all (138 feet [42 meters] from curb to curb), featuring tree-lined center medians that owe their design to the internationally famous French landscape architect Jean-Claude Nicolas Forestier, who was hired by the Machado government to undertake important works of city beautification.

The first lots of El Vedado were bought by well-to-do Havana families who decided to leave their mansions in the increasingly crowded old city and resettle in a nearby area that would be quieter and healthier. The oldest Vedado houses (some along Calle Línea) display neoclassical patterns derived from Palladian architecture. With the beginning of the Republic, patrician families and members of the new governing class took up residence in the growing suburb. The latter group included Generals Enrique Loynaz del Castillo and Domingo Méndez Capote, whose daughters Dulce María Loynaz and Renée Méndez Capote (both proud Vedadans and noted writers) left behind fundamental texts bearing witness to that era: Loynaz in interviews and notes toward a history, and Méndez Capote in her delight-ful autobiography *Las Memorias de una Cubanita que nació con el Siglo* (Memories of a Cuban Girl Who Was Born with the Century). The houses occu-pied by the Loynáz family not far from La Chorrera,

AVENUE OF ROYAL PALMS
OR PRESIDENT'S AVENUE,
HAVANA, CUBA

Avenida de los Presidentes, so-named for the monuments to past presidents erected along its central median, is one of the best-preserved streets in the country. Lately the median strip has been chosen by youthful fans of rock, reguetón, and other genres as a spot to gather nightly, share experiences, and sing.

VEDADO AVENUE AND TROTCHA HOTEL.

The Hotel Trotcha opened in 1883 as a function room but soon became Havana high society's favorite honeymoon hotel. The original neoclassical Salon was joined in 1902 by the Eden, a vernacular two-story wooden building, and in 1904 by the Washington, a picturesque three-story block. The Trotcha's hygienic qualities led the U.S. government to rent the hotel from 1899 to 1901 to house the high command of its occupation troops. Converted to a multifamily tenement in the 1930s, the Trotcha then suffered two fires, the final one devastating the buildings in 1986. All that remain standing today are the columns and pediment of the original Salon, a sad reminder for those who know of the hotel's former splendor. Surrounding this ruin, the city has recently constructed a grassy park.

Pedro Contreras 211

VEDADO Baños Street — Calle de Baños.

Calle E was formerly called Baños by the oldest residents of Vedado, who remembered when it led to the seaside El Progreso bathhouse, one of the rambling wooden structures built along the coral coast for sea-bathing. The Malecón now runs on top of the former bathhouse site, and only some foolhardy youths risk swimming off the Malecón and being dashed against the coral rock or seawall by the waves.

HABANA:—CALZADA DEL VEDADO.

VEDADO RESIDENCES AT CALZADA.

Along Calzada, a street running parallel to Línea and the seashore, stood and still stand some important residences built during the late nineteenth and early twentieth centuries, along with apartment buildings of varying quality constructed from the 1930s to the 1960s. Although two important buildings, the Hotel Presidente and the Teatro Auditorium, have recently been rehabilitated, this has not succeeded in restoring the street's former liveliness and charm.

The University of Havana sits at the top of a hill where Centro Habana meets El Vedado. It acquired its current appearance when the beautiful staircase was built in 1927. Since then, the university steps have been the scene of many important historical events, such as the first student torchlight march in honor of José Martí, which is commemorated every year. The university's facilities have now spread to other areas of the city with the building of new schools and divisions, but to Habaneros, "La Universidad" is still the cluster of buildings atop the hill.

in spite of their current ruinous state, still display the influence of the North American vernacular bungalow style. The residence where Renée Méndez Capote was born, still standing at the corner of Calles 15 and B, shows how the traditional Cuban home with a central courtyard changed under Anglo-Saxon influences to one where the courtyard was replaced by a wide passageway illuminated through a clerestory window of colored glass.

The First World War brought Cuba an era of rapid economic development thanks to soaring sugar prices on the world market. El Vedado reflected this boom in an accelerated growth of luxury residences of eclectic styles, such as that of the Marqueses de Avilés designed by the U.S. architect Thomas Hastings, or that of Pablo G. Mendoza by Leonardo Morales and his associate José Mata. In the early 1930s, two important high-rise buildings went up in Vedado: the imposing Hotel Nacional designed by McKim, Mead & White in homage to historical Spanish styles and constructed by Purdy & Henderson (see Chapter 10), and the Art Deco López Serrano apartment building, by the Cubans Mira and Rosich, with contours evocative of New York. In the late 1940s, the Modern Movement arrived in the form of new high-rises such as Radiocentro at Calle L and Calle 23, which anchored La Rampa, a new urban commercial center at the beginning of Calle 23 that was enlivened by outdoor art works. In 1963, coinciding with Havana's hosting of the Seventh Congress of the International Union of Architects, the new and architecturally audacious Pabellón Cuba opened to the public, helping to define La Rampa as the city's most modern and attractive area.

The radical social and economic changes brought to Cuba by the triumph of the Revolution spelled the ruin of an entire social class, the bourgeoisie, who left the country almost en masse when they saw their interests affected. The richest mansions of Vedado became state property and were turned to new uses. The Neo-Rococo French palace of the Countess Revilla de Camargo, decorated by the Casa Jansen, became the Museum of Decorative Arts. The house of Pedro Baró and Catalina Laza on Paseo, with its high Art Deco interior effects, has lost the strips of pure gold inlaid into the floor of its adjacent winter garden but retains the custom-made Lalique glass panes of its skylights and transoms; it is now the Casa de la Amistad (Friendship House). The noted architect and essayist Mario Coyula, a born-and-bred resident of Vedado, called attention to the negligence that threatens the area's status as a valuable example of urban design. Meanwhile, in an ancient mansion on Calle 5, Fichú Menocal Villalón (and Morales by marriage to her late husband, creating an assemblage of illustrious Vedado surnames) survives all the elements, including climatic ones that have forced her to raise the floor by more than a meter to protect against frequent sea floods. Every day she peeks out from her imposing front door to observe the lovely park built by her grandfather when he was minister of public works. In the bright sunshine, children noisily play baseball while lovers exchange caresses nearby.

FIFTH AVENUE AT MIRAMAR, HAVANA, CUBA

The main axis of the Miramar district, Quinta Avenida (Fifth Avenue) is famed for its garden-style median. It remains one of the most important boulevards of the city. The Fifth Avenue clock, symbol of Miramar and now of the municipality to which it belongs, was designed by an American, George H. Duncan.

12

ACROSS THE ALMENDARES

Felicia Chateloin

Marianao was dubbed "The City That Progresses" in a slogan of the 1950s, and indeed at that time it had a distinct identity that distinguished it from Havana.[1] Located within metropolitan Havana but across the Río Almendares from the city proper, it was the seat of a separate municipality.

When Cuba's current political-administrative divisions were adopted in 1976, the historical municipality of Marianao became three distinct municipalities or boroughs—Playa, Marianao, and La Lisa—out of the total of fifteen making up the juridical City of Havana. Playa ("beach") includes the coastal area stretching from the Almendares to Santa Fe; it forms a sort of continuation of El Vedado on the west side of the river. Marianao includes the central area, made up in general of the oldest neighborhoods. La Lisa is the inland area farther west, across the Río Quibú.

The urban design and architecture of these parts of modern Havana, with unique qualities dating from the colonial era and from more recent times, are representative of the manner of "making a city" that prevailed until the mid twentieth century, influenced especially by the concept of the "garden city." The three municipalities also contain an abandoned sugar mill, El Toledo; the remains of a horse-racing track; a dog-racing track now used for human sports; an old brewery, La Tropical, with its decayed adjacent beer gardens; a military base, Camp Columbia, transformed into a complex of schools (Ciudad Libertad); the capital's only complex embodying the monumental Modern style; the Plaza Finlay with its Obelisk of Marianao and surrounding buildings; a scattered network of commercial establishments matched only by that of Havana proper in the first

1. The slogan also appears on the current official shield of the municipality.

217

ALTURAS DE ALMENDARES PARK, HAVANA, CUBA

The 1930s saw the first moves to establish a park along the Almendares River. With the triumph of the Revolution in 1959, the Bosque de La Habana (Havana Woods) park was created under the arches of the Puente Almendares, as a public space offering fine landscape and environmental qualities. The 1960s were its period of greatest splendor.

Habana: Hipodromo, Carreras de Caballos.
Horse Racing, Grand Stand.

On January 14, 1915, the Hipódromo de Marianao (Marianao Horseracing Track) opened to the public at the corner of Avenida 63 and Calle 102, though not all of its facilities were yet complete. Cuban President Mario García Menocal attended the inauguration. The Casa Club opened in 1916, with the Jockey Club (the casino of Oriental Park, as the track was also known) on its first floor. The Oriental Park neighborhood grew up around these facilities. The track and casino closed in 1959, and in 1960 the buildings began to be remodeled. They now house a firm importing vehicle parts and transportation equipment (TRANSIMPORT, a division of Grupo UNECAMOTO)—a use not much in harmony with the original design. Some of the original characteristics survive, however, providing continued potential for future uses related to public performances or events.

Felicia Chateloin 219

Habana: Parque en el Reparto Miramar.
Miramar Park.

Parque Miramar stands on Quinta Avenida between Calle 22 and Calle 24.

half of the twentieth century; an astonishing number of now-shuttered movie theaters; Cuba's best and most internationally known cabaret, the Tropicana; the campus of the Instituto Superior de Arte (Arts College), one the most important achievements in Cuban architecture; the Ciudad Universitaria José Antonio Echeverría (CUJAE); the Centro Nacional de Investigaciones Científicas (CENIC); and an envi-

able natural environment with seacoast, beaches, rivers, and pleasant climate.

The first reports of this area tell of an indigenous territory called Mayanabo, to which many trace the origin of the modern name. In the eighteenth century, the separate villages of La Ceiba, Los Quemados, and Marianao grew up here, as did a road connecting them to each other and to Havana; in the nineteeth

century this became the Calzada Real, now Avenida 51. In 1830, a natural spring was discovered and developed in the Fuente de los Pocitos, whose reputation along with the new fad of river bathing attracted summer visitors.[2] The visitors in turn built *casas quintas* (rural estates) for temporary or permanent residence. In 1832, the Puente de La Lisa was constructed, the first span to bridge the Quibú.

The mid-nineteenth century saw an urban center grow up along the Calzada Real where the ruins of the Teatro Principal now stand. Toward 1860, the settlements of Los Quemados and Marianao merged and took the name of the latter. In 1861, the Calzada Real was improved from Puentes Grandes over the Almendares to the Puente de La Lisa over the Quibú. Two years later, the first railroad line to

2. The remains of the Fuente de los Pocitos may still be seen.

HABANA: PLAYA Y EDIFICIO DEL YACHT CLUB.

HAVANA YACHT CLUB AND BEACH.   106630

Havana Yacht Club was the first elite marina of the Playas de Marianao (Marianao beaches). The current building (located at Quinta Avenida and Calle 118), erected in 1924, replaced an earlier one dating from the late nineteenth century. Designed by Rafael Goyeneche and José Alejo Sánchez, the building now houses the Círculo Social Obrero Julio Antonio Mella (Julio Antonio Mella Workers' Social Club).

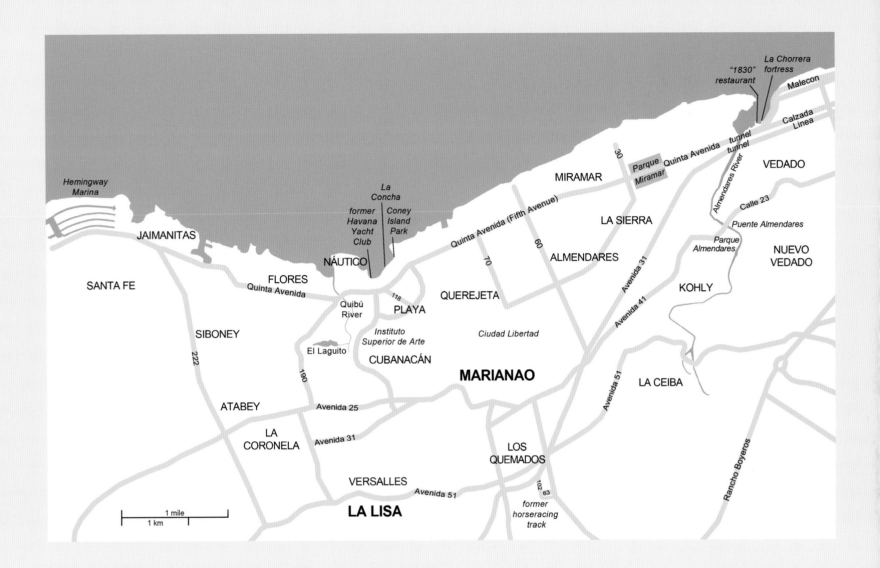

connect Havana and Marianao was completed. In 1864, a new avenue, the Calzada de La Playa, linked Marianao and the coastline. Toward the end of the century, stimulated partly by the early pollution of the Quibú, a new fad arose: bathing in the sea.

In 1878, coinciding with the division of Cuba into six provinces, the municipality of Marianao was born. Its geographical position adjoining the capital favored its development, while the status of the Almendares as the borderline underlined the place of Marianao's waterways in its identity.

At that time, the coastline was still nearly untouched, although the neighborhood of La Playa had begun to develop toward the end of the nineteenth century. The 1886 completion of the first building belonging to the "Sociedad Náutica Havana Yacht Club" marked the beginning of the Havana elite's appropriation of the coast.

Two names, Casino de La Playa and Casino Nacional, refer to the same institution, built in the 1920s in the area then known as Country Club. After some changes in the façade and some expansions, it adopted the name Casino Nacional. For nearly thirty years, it was regarded as Havana's most exclusive nightclub, attended by "the most distinguished Cuban and foreign visitors [and offering] splendid food, a gaming room, ballrooms, and its own house band." By 1956, it had closed, and the property on which it had stood became part of the Country Club golf course (hole 18). It stood more or less on Calle 120 between Avenida 11 and 11A, near today's School of Visual Arts at the Instituto Superior de Arte.

HABANA: CASINO DE LA PLAYA

THE NATIONAL CASINO AT MARIANAO

106673

HABANA: GRAN CASINO NACIONAL

·GRAN·CASINO·NACIONAL·

NATIONAL CASINO AT MARIANAO

OA4079

In 1956, this fountain was removed from its original location in the reflecting pool facing the Casino Nacional. It reappeared in the gardens of the Tropicana Night Club, which had been built some years before.

Marianao Bathing Beach

La Concha, built in 1922 to a design by the American architects Schultz and Weaver, was not an exclusive club. It was one of the few beaches open to the public; its customers, who came mostly from the middle classes, paid for each visit. Today it is called the Círculo Social Obrero Braulio Coroneaux (Braulio Coroneaux Workers' Social Club).

Cuba

Habana: Puente Almendares y Reparto Alturas
Almendares Bridge Vicinity

122977

The Puente Almendares (Almendares Bridge), also known as the Puente de Asbert, was built between 1905 and 1908, although it later had to be widened to accommodate growing automobile traffic. Connecting El Vedado with what is today the municipality of Playa, it provides access to Avenida 28, which borders the neighborhood called Alturas de Miramar (Miramar Heights), and connects with Avenida 47, which passes through Kohly.

The Hotel Almendares, built in the 1920s, was considered the most modern of the first-class Cuban hotels of its time. Advertisements compared it to the best U.S. hotels, with 200 rooms, outdoor terraces, ballrooms, a large jazz band, special transport service, golf courses, etc. By the 1940s, it had been converted to military uses related to the adjoining airport, housing the Military Aviation general staff. Constructed by Pablo Mendoza, the building lies within the former Camp Columbia (now Ciudad Libertad), at the corner of Calle 86 and Avenida 19 in Reparto Almendares within the municipality of Playa. It has undergone significant modification and today is a military zone.

Hotel Almendares, Havana, Cuba.—41

From the early twentieth century until the 1950s, the Playas de Marianao became an urban recreation zone, stimulated especially by the growth of tourism during the Prohibition era in the United States and continuing to expand thereafter. Facilities included bars, retail kiosks, nightclubs, hotels, cafeterias and restaurants, gambling casinos, private clubs, golf courses, dance halls, and even "puestos de fritas" (hamburger stands). The ambiance of these establishments varied greatly. In the exclusive private clubs, the elite played golf and tennis and even boarded cruise ships; varying among themselves in their degrees of elitism, these enclaves included the Yacht Club, the Casino Español, the

Daughters of Galicia, the Hardware Dealers' Club, and the Club Náutico. Other spaces offered recreation to a variety of social classes; these included La Concha swimming pool, Coney Island amusement park, and even some "dancing schools" that were actually fronts for prostitution. The strongest suits of the foreign tourist trade were gambling, music, and dance.

Famous bands played in the upper-class clubs and casinos, where the dominant form was ballroom dancing to both U.S. and Cuban tunes. In La Playa, on the other hand, Cuban popular music continually evolved through the performance of rumba, son, jazz, and various kinds of fusion. Among the itin-

26   A SCENE IN COUNTRY CLUB PARK, HAVANA, CUBA.   110653

Created to promote the playing of golf, the Country Club opened its clubhouse in 1911, thus spurring development of the suburb called Country Club Park. The neighborhood's design and construction were in the hands of the Frederick Snare Corporation and the architect T. Newton. Once the retreat of millionaires, the neighborhood now houses mostly diplomatic facilities. It has also been called El Laguito because of a small lake fed by the Río Quibú, surrounded by luxury residences; this area is not open to the public.

erant and well-known musicians who congregated there were Beny Moré, Manuel Corona, Miguelito Valdés, and "El Chori," a drummer of mythic stature who filled the streets of Havana with graffiti bearing his name. Among the hot spots of La Playa nightlife were venues like the Pennsylvania, the Rumba Palace, El Panchín, and El Niche.

One factor that aided the area's development was continued road and rail building and the expansion of transportation. The Calzada Real, as an extension of the Calzada de Puentes Grandes, now reached all the way to the province of Pinar del Río. The Puente Almendares (also known as the Asbert) was built between 1905 and 1908 to link El Vedado and Marianao, followed in 1921 by a second bridge, the Puente de Pote, which joined El Vedado's Calle Calzada to Quinta Avenida (Fifth Avenue) in Miramar. By 1926, Quinta Avenida had been extended to La Playa, and in 1942 it reached farther west to Jaimanitas. In 1958, today's Calzada Tunnel replaced the former bridge. Meanwhile, the Puente de Línea had replaced the aged Puente de Ibañez, allowing streetcars to cross from Vedado to Marianao, and in 1953 it, too, was replaced by a tunnel, the Túnel de Línea of today. Avenida 31 opened in 1955, followed in 1988 by Avenida 25, which linked Avenida 31 to the Autopista del Mediodía.

G 12063 a. Residence of American Minister - Residencia del Ministro Americano, Marianao, Cuba.

Since the mid-twentieth century, the overall urban design of the area has not changed very much. With a few exceptions left from the colonial period, the architecture ranges from eclecticism to the Modern Movement. Many of the original place names remain in use (including those of the old centers of Marianao, Los Quemados, and La Ceiba as well as the many newer ones from the first half of the twentieth century), although the boundaries of these neighborhoods, as understood in the popular usage of the names, have changed. Neighborhoods in the current municipality of Marianao include Zamora (1862), Pogolotti, the first Cuban development specifically for the working class (1912), and Buen Retiro (1912); the area around the former racetrack, originally known as Oriental Park (1917), is now referred to simply as Oriental. The current municipality of Playa includes Buenavista and Almendares (1904), Miramar (with all its extensions, 1911–1940s), Kohly (1912), La Sierra (1916), Querejeta (1918), La Coronela (1928), Náutico (1946), Flores (1947), and La Puntilla (1954). Some names in Playa have officially been changed: Biltmore (1942) to Siboney, Alturas de Biltmore (1950s) to Atabey, and Country Club (1916) to Cubanacán; El Romerillo persists unaltered. In the modern municipality of La Lisa, which contains the poorest population of the three, surviving

This mansion, which served as the U.S. ambassador's residence, was located on Avenida 51, previously the Calzada Real. Now greatly transformed and subdivided, it is nearly unrecognizable, having lost part of the main façade, the entranceway, and the front yard fencing when the street was widened and straightened early in the twentieth century.

names include Alturas de La Lisa (1945), Versalles (1950), and Balcón de La Lisa (1952); alongside the Río Quibú, names of marginal settlements like La Korea remain in use as well.

The building stock is practically the same as the area had in the 1950s, although it is in worse condition in the municipalities of Marianao and La Lisa, while Playa can boast some of the best conditions in the city of Havana. Important changes in function have occurred since 1960, such as the depressed state of the traditional commercial center of Marianao (Avenida 51) on the one hand, and the transformation of the former residential zone of Miramar into an area of commercial, institutional, tourist, and other new uses on the other hand. The former private clubs are public areas today.

Havana grew more by addition than by replacement and managed to modernize without violating its essence as a city caressed by the sea and embraced by the river. From its founding to the present, Havana has been favored by a historical arc from village to city, until it could realize the dream of every provincial settlement: to become a capital in its own right. Havana is more than words can capture. Its beauty outweighs its deterioration. Havana waits impatiently for the changes of the twenty-first century, for transformation understood as development, for restoration carried out with love and care.

REPÚBLICA DE CUBA
TARJETA POSTAL
UNION POSTALE UNIVERSELLE
1906

NOS VENDETA TOBAGO
COMPRE AZUCAR
Post Card
OUR LARGEST
BE OUR LARGEST SUPPLIER
BUY CUBAN SUGAR

REPÚBLICA DE CUBA
TARJETA POSTAL
UNION POSTALE UNIVERSELLE

HABANA
DIC 22
3 PM
CUBA

HABANA·CUBA
DIC 3
11 PM
1906

Mrs. R. M. Blackerby
1710. Edwar

A Mlle. Antoinette Luiny
Laforja 11 Torre
San Gervas
Barcelona

UNION POSTAL
POST-C

Impresos
½
República de Cuba
Tarjeta Postal — Post-Card

Edición Jordi.

I hear you are home-
ward bound hope you
had a good time.
Write me once in a while
and tell me what kind

Leopoldo
ygo

Ver

Rep. Argentina
Mr Arnaldo Ghisla
Avenida Mayo 1341
Buenos Aires

Mailing Card
CARTE POSTALE

HAVANA
FEB 8
11 PM
CUBA

Navia
(Montevid
(Uruguay)

This side is exclusively for the adress

REPÚBLICA DE CUBA
TARJETA POSTAL
UNION POSTALE UNIVERSELLE

GUIDO DAMA, Industria 138. HABANA

HABANA·CUBA
ABR 27
9 AM
1904

Señ ra M. Gallese M.
Arzobispo #2 Lima
Peru

En este lado se escribe solamente la Dirección.

Partos y Ginecología de los Dres A.S.
Bustamente y Enrique Nuñez, Calle J (Vedado)
Habana, Cuba.

Solamente para la dirección

Pompilio Mule
La Academ
Sagua la
G de

Coimbra
S. Frutuozo
Portugal

from Selly
or B.B.

CARD.
CARD. CARTE POSTALE.

Siebert
little wife.

Place Postage
Stamp Here
Domestic and
Canada
One Cent
Foreign
Two Cents

Söderköping

ABOUT THE CONTRIBUTORS

Cathryn Griffith is a graduate of Wellesley College and the School of the Museum of Fine Arts in Boston, Massachusetts, where she makes her home. She has made more than a dozen working trips to Havana since her first journey there in 2003. A student of French culture and language, she has written and lectured about the Musée d'Orsay. She has photographed in many places, including New England, France, China, Tibet, and across the Silk Road.

Dick Cluster (translator) has translated novels, stories, and essays by Cuban and other writers for publishers including City Lights, St. Martins, Beacon, Bulfinch, University of Florida, and more. He is the author of *The History of Havana* (with Rafael Hernández), three novels, and additional books of popular history and economics. He translated all the text by Cuban writers.

Eusebio Leal Spengler (Foreword), the driving force behind the restoration of Havana, became director of the Museum of the City of Havana and subsequently was named Historian of the City and president of its Monuments Commission. He oversaw restoration of many of Havana's major buildings, including the Governors' Palace, Fortress of La Cabaña, and Morro Castle. He has written prolifically about the history of Cuba and has been recognized internationally with many prizes, awards, and honors for his work in restoring Havana.

Felix Julio Alfonso López (Chapter 1), who holds degrees in history, sociocultural anthropology, and interdisciplinary studies on Latin America, works on the Master Plan for the city of Havana in the Office of the Historian of the City of Havana. The author of several publications, he has taught and participated in conferences on the history and preservation of Havana in the United Kingdom and Latin America.

Felicia Chateloin Santiesteban (Chapter 12) is an architect, historian, and critic, and specializes in restoration. President of the Technical Commission for Patrimony of the Union of Architects and Engineers of the Construction of Cuba (UNAICC) and author of numerous publications, she teaches at the Faculty of Architecture and works in the Office of the Historian of the City of Havana.

Pedro Contreras Suárez (Chapter 11) is an art historian and graphic designer devoted to research and the promotion of Cuban design at the Center for the Development of Visual Arts, where he has curated exhibitions of contemporary Cuban art. He has written for the Cuban cultural press and is the author of several books, including *Havana Deco* (W. W. Norton, 2007). He was one of the winners of the National Prize for Curatorship in 2008.

Leland Cott, FAIA (Chapter 9), is a founding principal of Bruner/Cott & Associates, Architects and Planners, in Cambridge, Massachusetts, and adjunct professor of Urban Design at the Harvard Graduate School of Design, where he has taught design studios concentrating on sites in Havana. In 2006 he helped lead the successful effort to preserve and reconstruct Ernest Hemingway's house, the Finca Vigía, in San Francisco de Paula, Cuba. His current interests are focused on the protection and preservation of Havana's mid-twentieth-century landmarks.

Mario Coyula Cowley (Introduction, Chapters 3, 8, and 10) is an architect, urban planner, critic, and author of numerous publications. Now Distinguished Professor, he was Havana's director of Architecture and Urban Planning, director of the School of Architecture, and first president of the Commission on Historical Monuments. He received the National Architecture Prize for lifetime achievement (2001) and the National Prize for Habitat (2004). He was Robert F. Kennedy Visiting Professor at the Harvard University Graduate School of Design in 2002, and Invited Professor at the Angewandte of Vienna in 2006.

Orestes M. del Castillo del Prado (Chapter 6) is professor emeritus at the Havana School of Architecture. He holds a doctorate in architecture and, as consulting architect and technical adviser in the Office of the Historian from 1995 to 2008, directed the rehabilitation of the Produce Exchange in the Plaza de San Francisco and other important buildings in Old Havana.

Lillian Guerra (Chapter 7) is the author of *Visions of Power: Revolution and Redemption in Cuba* (2010); *The Myth of José Martí* (2005), and *Popular Expression and National Identity in Puerto Rico* (1998). She has also published many scholarly articles, essays, and two

collections of Spanish-language poetry. The U.S. born scholar teaches Caribbean and modern Latin American history at Yale University.

Silvia María Morales Pérez (Chapter 2) is an architect. Graduate of the Faculty of Architecture, her field of study was the military, religious, and civil buildings of Havana's Historic Center, where she worked as a specialist for three years. She is currently studying for a master's degree in restoration of architectural patrimony at the Polytechnic University of Catalonia.

Daniel M. Taboada Espiniella (Chapter 4), an architect, won the National Award in Architecture and First Prize for an architect in public service in 1998 and in 2005 received the highest honor granted by the International Federation of American and European Preservation Centers (CICOP) for "his career and work in favor of preservation of the Cuban architectural and cultural heritage in the world."

Carlos Venegas Fornias (Chapter 5) is an art historian specializing in the urban history and architecture of Cuba. He has worked at the Ministry of Culture in the field of conservation and restoration since 1978; he now concentrates on the history of daily life and material culture in colonial Havana. He is the author of articles and books on these subjects both in Cuba and abroad.

BIBLIOGRAPHY

Alonso, Alejandro G., Pedro Contreras, and Martino Fagiuoli. *Havana Deco*. New York: W. W. Norton, 2007.

Blanes Martín, Tamara. *Castillo de los Tres Reyes del Morro de La Habana: Historia y Arquitectura*. La Habana: Editorial Letras Cubanas, 1998.

———. *Fortificaciones del Caribe*. La Habana: Editorial Letras Cubanas, 2001.

———. "Un acercamiento hacia las principales fortificaciones coloniales de Cuba," in *Revista de Historia Militar* 99. Madrid: Instituto de Historia y Cultura Militar, 2006.

Cluster, Dick, and Rafael Hernández. *The History of Havana*. New York: Palgrave Macmillan, 2008.

Cuevas Toraya, Juan de las. *500 años de construcciones en Cuba*. Madrid: Chavín, 2001.

Evans, Walker. *Havana 1933*. New York: Pantheon, 1989.

Félix de Arrate, José Martín. *Llave del Nuevo Mundo. Antemural de las Indias Occidentales. La Habana descripta, noticias de su fundación, aumentos y estado*. La Habana: Comisión Nacional Cubana de La UNESCO, 1964.

Fernández Santalicio, Manuel. *Las antiguas iglesias de La Habana. Tiempo vida y semblante*. Miami: Ediciones Universal, 1997.

González, Mario. "El Malecón habanero. Apuntes histórico-conceptuales," in *Carta de La Habana*. La Habana: Grupo para el Desarrollo Integral de la Capital, August 1993.

Guerra, Lillian. *The Myth of José Martí: Conflicting Nationalisms in Early Twentieth-Century Cuba*. Chapel Hill: University of North Carolina Press, 2005.

———. *Visions of Power: Revolution and Redemption in Cuba, 1952–1972*. Chapel Hill: University of North Carolina Press, 2010.

Jiménez García, Eduardo, and José A. Domínguez Granda. "El Trotcha. Semblanza de un gigante," in *Arquitectura Cuba* 378, La Habana, 1998.

Journal of Decorative and Propaganda Arts, No. 22: Cuba Theme Issue 1875–1945. Miami: Wolfson Foundation of Decorative and Propaganda Arts, 1996.

Leal Spengler, Eusebio. *Detén el paso caminante*. La Habana: Letras Cubanas, 1988.

———. *La Habana, ciudad antigua*. La Habana: Letras Cubanas, 1988.

———. *Regresar en el tiempo*. La Habana: Letras Cubanas, 1986.

Loynaz, Dulce María. *Fe de Vida*. La Habana: Letras Cubanas, 2000.

Martín, María Elena, and Eduardo Luis Rodríguez. *La Habana. Guía de Arquitectura*. Seville: Junta de Andalucía, 1998.

Rodríguez, Eduardo Luis. *La Habana. Arquitectura del Siglo XX*. Barcelona: Blume, 1998.

———. *The Havana Guide: Modern Architecture, 1925–1965*. New York: Princeton Architectural Press, 2000.

Rodríguez, Eduardo Luis, and María Elena Martín: *La Habana. Map and guide to 337 significant architectural monuments*. Darmstadt, Germany: Editorial Trialog, 1992.

Scarpaci, Joseph L., Mario Coyula, and Roberto Segre. *Havana: Two Faces of the Antillean Metropolis*. Chapel Hill: University of North Carolina Press, 2002.

Segre, Roberto. *La Plaza de Armas de La Habana. Sinfonía urbana inconclusa*. La Habana: Editorial Arte y Literatura, 1995.

Taylor, Henry Louis, Jr. *Inside El Barrio: A Bottom-up View of Neighborhood Life in Castro's Cuba*. Sterling, VA: Kumarian Press, 2009.

Venegas Fornias, Carlos. *La urbanización de Las Murallas: dependencia y modernidad*. La Habana: Letras Cubanas, 1989.

———. "El Malecón habanero," in *Revolución y Cultura*, La Habana, July-August, 1994.

———. *Plazas de intramuro*. La Habana: Consejo Nacional de Patrimonio Cultural, 2003.

Weiss, Joaquín E. *La arquitectura colonial cuban*. La Habana-Seville: Instituto Cubano del Libro, 1996.

INDEX

Note: Page numbers in italic type indicate illustrations.

Abad y Valdés-Navarrete, Antonio, 76
Abarca, Silvestre, 43
Abraham Lincoln monument, *133, 137*
Acera del Louvre café, 154
Acera del Louvre (Louvre sidewalk), 154
Aguas Claras mansion. *See* Marqueses de Aguas
    Claras mansion
Alameda de Isabel II, 161
Albear y Fernández de Lara, Francisco de, 103,
    108, 112, 177
Alejo Sánchez, José, 222
Almendares, 230
Almendares Bridge. *See* Puente Almendares
El Almendares optical shop, *110,* 112
Almendares River. *See* Río Almendares
Alonso, Alicia, 155
Alturas de Biltmore, 230
Alturas de La Lisa, 231
Alturas de Miramar (Miramar Heights), 227
American Club, 172
Amigó, Arturo, 172
Antonelli, Bautista, 40, 177
Arco de Belén, *112,* 112
Art Deco, 15, 185, 215
Art Nouveau, 15
Arteaga, Cardinal Manuel, 78
Asturian Club. *See* Centro Asturiano
Atabey, 230
Augustine friars, 83, 87
Autopista del Mediodía, 229
Avenida 25, 229
Avenida 28, 227
Avenida 31, 229
Avenida 47, 227
Avenida 51, 221, *231. See also* Calzada Real
Avenida de los Presidentes (Avenue of the Presi-
    dents), 207, *209*
Avenida del Puerto, 55, 184
Avenida Maceo, *174, 196*
Avenida Simón Bolívar, *91, 126,* 128
Avenue of the Presidents. *See* Avenida de los
    Presidentes
Avilés, Marqueses de, 215

Balcón de La Lisa, 231
Ballet Nacional de Cuba, 155
Barclay, Parsons & Klapp, 65
Baró, Pedro, 215
Baroque style, 13, 24, 76, 79–82, 88
Baterí Santa Clara, 184
bathing pools, 192
Batista, Eugenio, 146

Batista, Fulgencio, 135
Beaux Arts style, 15
Belau, Paul, 156, 187
Belén Arch. *See* Arco de Belén
Beller, Darden, 164
Bens Arrarte, José María, 139
Bethlemite Friars, 112
Biltmore, 230
Bolívar, Simón, 131, *133*
bone pile, 97, *99*
Boni, Domenico, 186
Borges Recío, Max, 197
Bosque de La Habana (Havana Woods), *218*
Braulio Coroneaux Workers' Social Club. *See*
    Círculo Social Obrero Braulio Coroneaux
Breakers, Palm Beach, Florida, 186
Brun, Charles, 167
Buen Retiro, 230
Buenavista, 230
Busto, Manuel del, 156

Caballero de Paris (Villa Soberón), *60*
La Cabaña, 39, *41,* 42, *52*
Cabarrocas, Félix, 29, 139, 178
Calixto García monument, *193*
Calle 17, *204*
Calle 23 (La Rampa),178, 207
Calle Aguiar, 103
Calle Ancha, 161
Calle Calzada, 229
Calle Colón, 165
Calle Crespo, 177
Calle Cuba, 103
Calle de Baños, *212*
Calle de Empedrado, 71, 76, *105*
Calle E, 192, *212*
Calle G, 184, 186, 192, 207. *See also* Avenida de
    los Presidentes
Calle Galiano, 140
Calle Habana, 103
Calle Línea, 207–8, *208*
Calle Neptuno, 140, *158,* 165
Calle O, *206*
Calle Obispo, 103, *107, 111,* 112, 140
Calle Oficios, 55, 66
Calle O'Reilly, 103, *104, 106,* 140
Calle Salud, 88
Calle San Ignacio, 71, 76
Calle San Lázaro, 92, 165, *170,* 177
Calle San Rafael, 140
Calle Sierpes, Seville, Spain, 103
Callejón del Chorro, 71, 76

Calona, Francisco de, 39
Calzada de Belascoaín, 178
Calzada de La Playa, 223
Calzada de la Reina, 90, *100*
Calzada de Medina, 178
Calzada de Monte (Monte Street), 121, 128, 146
Calzada del Vedado, *213*
Calzada Máximo Gómez, 128
Calzada Real, 221, 229. *See also* Avenida 51
Calzada Tunnel, 229
Camp Columbia, 217, 228
La Capilla de la Fortaleza de San Carlos de la
    Cabaña, *48*
Capitol Building, Washington, D.C., *136*
Capitolio Nacional, 29, 123, 133, 135, *136, 138,*
    139, *140–43,* 161
Carlos III, King of Spain, 43, 71
Carlos Manuel de Céspedes (López Mesa), 29
El Carmelo, 201
El Carmelo (restaurant), 207
Carneado bathing pool, 192
carnival performers, 116, *117, 118* (detail)
Casa Bayona mansion. *See* Condes de Casa
    Bayona mansion
Casa Club, 219
Casa de Baños, 76, 77
Casa de Correos, 24
Casa de la Amistad (Friendship House), 215
Casa Jansen, 215
Casino de La Playa, *224*
Casino Español (Spanish Club), 167, *168,* 172, 228
Casino Nacional (National Casino), *224, 225*
Castillo de la Chorrera. *See* Santa Dorotea de
    Luna de la Chorrera Fortress
Castillo de la Punta fortress, 146, *174,* 177, 195
Castillo de la Real Fuerza de la Habana, 13, 19,
    20, 21, 23, 24, 29, 39, *52,* 184
Castillo de los Tres Reyes del Morro (castle of the
    three kings of the *morro*), 39–40, *40–42,*
    42, *48,* 161
Castillo, Orestes del, 65
Cathedral of Havana, 70, 71, *73, 74,* 76, *78–79,*
    78–79
Cathedral of Seville, 79
Cathedral of the Santísima Trinidad (Holy Trin-
    ity), 88, *89*
Catholicism, 81, 83, 87, 90
La Ceiba, 220, 230
ceiba trees, 24, *36,* 36, 131, *132,* 135
Cementerio de Colón (Columbus Cemetery), 92,
    93–99, 95, *97,* 208
Cementerio Espada, *92,* 92

Central Park. *See* Parque Central
Central Railway Station, *119*
Centro Asturiano (Asturian Club), *156*, 156, *157*, 172
Centro de Dependientes del Comercio (Commercial Employees' Center), 172, *173*
Centro de Restauración Museológica, 83
Centro Gallego (Galician Center), 152, *153–55*, 156, 172
Centro Habana, 139, 140, 161, 195
Centro Hispano-Americano de Cultura (Spanish-American Cultural Center), 180
Centro Histórico, 103, 112, 114, 116, 119
Centro Nacional de Investigaciones Científicas (CENIC), 220
Céspedes, Carlos Manuel de, *29*, 29, 202
Changó, 135
Chapel of the Third Order, 55
"El Chori," 229
La Chorrera. *See* Santa Dorotea de Luna de La Chorrera Fortress
Christina's Market. *See* Mercado de Cristina
Christopher Columbus (Cuchiari), *33*, 35
Church and Convent of San Francisco de Asís (St. Francis of Assisi), *54*, 55, 56, *58–59*, *61*
Church of the Good Journey. *See* Iglesia del Santo Cristo del Buen Viaje
Church of the Holy Trinity. *See* Cathedral of the Santísima Trinidad
Churriguera, José de, 88
Churrigueresque style, 88
cigar box label, *124*
Círculo Social Obrero Braulio Coroneaux (Braulio Coroneaux Workers' Social Club), 226
Círculo Social Obrero Julio Antonio Mella (Julio Antonio Mella Workers' Social Club), 222
city walls, *102*
Ciudad Libertad, 217, 228
Ciudad Universitaria José Antonio Echeverría (CUJAE), 220
Club Náutico, 228
Colegio Universitario San Gerónimo de La Habana, *104*
colonial Baroque, 81
Columbus Cemetery. *See* Cementerio de Colón
Columbus, Christopher, 33, 35, 78–79, 131
Columbus Market. *See* Mercado de Colón
Columbus Memorial Chapel. *See* El Templete
Columbus Park. *See* Parque de Colón
La Concha, 226, 228
Conde de Lombillo (Lombillo mansion), 73, 75
Conde de Lombillo mansion (Lombillo mansion), 72, 76
Condes de Casa Bayona mansion, 75, 77
Congregación de la Misión, 87
Congress of the International Union of Architects, 215
Convent of Santa Clara, *83*, 83
Coolidge, Calvin, 131
Corona, Manuel, 229
La Coronela, 230
Country Club, 224, *229*, 230

Coyula, Mario, 215
Cristo del Buen Viaje, 81
Cuarteles Street, *104*
Cuba (ship), *175*
Cuban Baroque, 13
Cuban Institute of Friendship among the People (ICAP), 204
Cuban National Opera, 155
Cuban Telephone Company, *129*
Cubanacán, 230
Cuchiari, J., *Christopher Columbus*, *33*, 35
Cuendias, José, 195
Custom House, *54*, *57*, *63–65*, *65–66*

Daughter of Galicia, 228
Las Delicias bathing pool, 192
Las Delicias de Medina (restaurant), 207
Department of Public Works, 83
El Diario de la Marina (newspaper), 150
Domínguez, Nelson, 56
Dos Hermanos (Two Brothers) bar, *66*, 66
Droguería Johnson, *110*, 112
Duncan, George H., 216
Durnford, Elias, 24

Eden (Hotel Trotcha), 211
1830 restaurant, 202
Embarcadero, San Francisco, USA, 66
Embassy of Spain, 188
Embassy of Switzerland, *186*, 186
El Encanto bathing pool, 192
entierros (burial parades), 92, 99, *100*, *101*
Episcopalians, 88
La Escalinata, 140
Escuela Primaria Especial (Special Primary School) Emma Rosa Chuy, 166
Espada, Bishop, 24
Esquina Caliente (Hot Corner), 146, *147*
La Estatua de la República (Statue of the Republic) (Zanelli), 139, *142*
estilos de devoción, 81

Farmacia Taquechel, 112
Félix de Arrate, José Martín, 24
Fernández, Rómulo, 195
Fernando VII, King of Spain, *29*, 29
Fifth Avenue. *See* Quinta Avenida
Fireman Monument (Querol and Zapata), *97*, 97
First Avenue. *See* Primera Avenida
First Presbyterian Church. *See* Iglesia Presbiteriana
Flores, 230
FOCSA building, *197*
Fondesviela, Felipe, Marqués de la Torre, 24
Forestier, Jean-Claude Nicolas, 73, 139, 161, 184, 208
Fortaleza de San Carlos de la Cabaña (Fortress of the Cabaña), 43, *45–51*, 45, 48, *53*
Fountain of the Lions. *See* Fuente de los Leones
La Francia department store, 112
Franciscan friars, 81, 87
Francisco de Albear statue (Vilalta de Saavedra),

108
Fraternity Park. *See* Parque de la Fraternidad Americana
Frederick Snare Corporation, 229
Fuente de La India (Fountain of La India), 133, *134*. See also *La India* (Gaggini)
Fuente de la Juventud, 195
Fuente de los Leones (Fountain of the Lions), 66, *67–69*, 133
Fuente de los Pocitos, *221*, 221
La Fuerza Fort. *See* Castillo de la Real Fuerza de la Habana
funerary rites, 92, 99, *100*, *101*

Gaggini, Giuseppe, 66, 133
   La India, 131
Galería de Tobías (Tobias's Gallery), 97, *98*
Gamba, Aldo, 186
García, Calixto, 192, 193
García Menocal, Mario, 219
garden cities, 217
La Giralda, Seville, Spain, 119
La Giraldilla de la Habana, 23
Gogorza, Brother Luís, 90
Gómez, Joaquín, 112
Gómez, José Miguel, 123, *125*, 167
Gómez, Máximo, 131, 186, 188
Gómez Sampera, Ernesto, 197
González de Adalid, Javier, 56, 65
Goodhue, Bertram Grosvenor, 88
Gothic style, 88, 90. *See also* Neo-Gothic style
Govantes, Evelio, 29, 139
Governors' Palace. *See* Palacio de los Capitanes Generales
Goyeneche, Rafael, 222
Gran Teatro de la Habana, 155
Granda, Félix, 91
Greek Orthodox Cathedral of San Nicolás de Mira, 55, *60*
Grupo UNECAMOTO, 219

La Habana Vieja (Old Havana), 15, 19, 81, 103, *105*, 112, 114, 116, 119, 139
Hallet, Étienne-Sulpice, 92
Hardware Dealers' Club, 228
Hastings, Thomas, 215
Havana, 13–15, *14*, *16–17*, 19, 39
Havana Central Railroad Company, 83
Havana Harbor Tunnel, 48
Havana Radio, 62
Havana Yacht Club, *222*
Henie, Sonja, 195
Hermanos Ameijeiras Hospital, *189*
Herrera, Juan de, 7
Herrerian style, 7
Hipódromo de Marianao (Marianao Horseracing Track), *219*
historicist architecture, 81
Horizontal Property Law, 197
Hot Corner. *See* Esquina Caliente
Hotel Almendares, *228*
Hotel Florida, 112

Hotel Inglaterra, 146, *147–49*, *152*, *153*, 154
Hotel Miramar, 177
Hotel Nacional, 184, *185*, 186, 215
Hotel Parque Central, 157, *158*
Hotel Plaza, *144*, *150*, *151*, 154, *158*
Hotel Presidente, 213
Hotel Saratoga, *130*
Hotel Sevilla Biltmore, 169
Hotel Telégrafo, *147*, *149*, 154
Hotel Trotcha, *210*, 211
House of Austria, 20
Hubbard, Elbert, *A Message to Garcia*, 193

ICAP (Cuban Institute for Friendship among the Peoples), 204
Iglesia de San Francisco, *86* (detail), *87*, 87
Iglesia de San Francisco de Paula, *82*, 83
Iglesia del Sagrado Corazón (Church of the Sacred Heart), Centro Habana, 90, *91*, *128*
Iglesia del Sagrado Corazón (Church of the Sacred Heart), Vedado, 90
Iglesia del Santo Cristo del Buen Viaje (Church of the Good Journey), *80*, 81
Iglesia del Vedado, 90
Iglesia Parroquial Mayor, 19, 71
Iglesia Presbiteriana (First Presbyterian Church), *88*, 88
La India (Gaggini), 131, *135*. *See also* Fuente de la India
Instituto Superior de Arte (Arts College), 220, 224
Isabella II, Queen of Spain, 129

Jaimanitas, 229
Janua sum Pacis (I am the doorway to peace) (Vilalta de Saavedra), 92, *93*, 95
El Jardín (restaurant), 207
Jesuits, 90, 112
Jockey Club, 219
John Paul II, Pope, 79
José Martí statue (Vilalta de Saavedra), *120*, 140, *146*
José Miguel Gómez house, *167*, 167
Juan Clemente Zenea memorial, *164*, 165
Juárez, Benito, *133*
Julio Antonio Mella Workers' Social Club. *See* Círculo Social Obrero Julio Antonio Mella

King Fernando VII (Solá), 29
Kohly, 227, 230
La Korea, 231

El Laguito, 229
lampposts, Paseo del Prado, *165*, 165
Las Casas, Bartolomé de, 39
Lawton, 15
Laza, Catalina, 215
Lincoln, Abraham, *133*, *137*
Línea. *See* Calle Línea
lion sculptures, Paseo del Prado, *164*, 165
La Lisa, 217, *223*, 231
Loira, Calixto de, 92, *93*

Lombillo mansion. *See* Conde de Lombillo mansion
Lonja de Comercio (Produce Exchange), *53*, 56, *62*, *63*, 65–66
López Mesa, Sergio, *Carlos Manuel de Céspedes*, 29
López Serrano apartment building, 215
Loynaz del Castillo, Enrique, 208
Loynaz, Dulce María, 208

Maceo, Antonio, 121, 186, 192
Maceo Park. *See* Parque y Monumento a Maceo
Machado, Gerardo, 123, 131, 133, 135, 208
La Machina, *61*
Maine. See U.S.S. *Maine*
Malecón, 161, *174*, 177–78, *178–94*, 184, 186, 192, 195, *196–99*, 197
Manzana de Gómez (Gómez Block), 140, *144*, *145*
Marianao, 217, 220, 221, *223*, 223, 229–31
Marianao beaches. *See* Playas de Marianao
marmolerías, 95
Marqueses de Aguas Claras mansion, 76, 77
Marqueses de Arcos mansion, *73*, 75
Martí, José, *120*, 121, 131, 135, 140, 192, 214
Martínez Márquez, Cristóbal, 78
Martínez Piloto family residence, *206*
Maruri, Carlos, 156, 187
Mata, José, 154, 215
Maumejean, 91
Maximilian, Emperor of Mexico, 133
Máximo Gómez monument, 186, *188*
Mayanabo, 220
Mazariegos, Diego de, 40
McKim, Mead & White, 184, 215
Memorial a los Estudiantes de Medicina (Medical Students' Memorial), *179*
Méndez Capote, Domingo, 208
Méndez Capote, Renée, 215
    Las Memorias de una Cubanita que nació con el Siglo, 208
Mendoza, Pablo G., 215, 228
Menocal, Mario, 123
Menocal Villalón, Fichú, 215
Mensa, Alessandro, 66
El Mercado, *113*, *114*
Mercado de Colón (Columbus Market), *113*, 114
Mercado de Cristina (Christina's Market), *113*, 114
Mercedarian Order, 87
Meucci, Antonio, 156
Mexican Baroque style, 88
Ministerio de Ciencia, Tecnología y Medio Ambiente (Ministry of Science, Technology and the Environment), 138
Mira and Rosich, 215
Miramar, 197, *216*, 230, 231
Miramar Heights. *See* Alturas de Miramar
Miramar Park. *See* Parque en el Reparto Miramar
La Moderna Poesía (Modern Poetry) building, *111*, 112
modernism, 15, 215

Moneo, Rafael, 164
Monserrate Gate, 139
Monte Street. *See* Calzada de Monte
Morales and Mata, 205
Morales, Leonardo, 215
Moré, Beny, 229
Morrish-Spanish style, 185
Morro-Cabaña Military Historical Park, 48, *49*
Morro Castle. *See* Castillo de los Tres Reyes del Morro
Mudéjar style, 13, 80
Mur, Tomás, 56
Murchison, Kenneth, 119
Museo de Arte Colonial, 77
Museo de la Ciudad (Museum of the City), 24, 32
Museo de la Revolución, 186, *187*
Museo de San Salvador de La Punta, 178
Museo Nacional de Bellas Artes (National Museum of Fine Arts), *113*
Museum of Decorative Arts, 215

Napoleon III, 133
Naranjo, Paulino, 188
Narváez, Pánfilo de, 39
National Archive, 29
National Casino. *See* Casino Nacional
National Library, 29
National Union of Cuban Writers and Artists (UNEAC), 204
Náutico, 230
Neo-Gothic style, 13–14, 81, 90
Neo-Rococo, 215
neoclassical style, 14, 24, 92, 185, 208
neocolonial style, 185
Newton, T., 229
El Niche, 229
Nuestra Señora de la Merced, 83, *84*, *85* (detail), 87
Iglesia de San Francisco, 83

Obelisk of Marianao, 217
El Océano bathing pool, 192
O'Donnell, Leopoldo, 42
O'Donnell Lighthouse, 42–43, *43*, *44* (detail)
Office of the Historian of the City of Havana, 10, 36, 60, 72
Old Havana. *See* La Habana Vieja
Oriental, 230
Oriental Park. *See* Hipódromo de Marianao
Otero, Raúl, 139, 161
Our Lady of Loreto, 79

Pabellón Cuba, 215
Packard Hotel, 164, *175*
Palacio de Bellas Artes, 114
Palacio de los Capitanes Generales (Governors' Palace), *6*, *7*, 24, *25–28*, 29, *32–36*, 35–36, 119
Palacio de los Deportes, 195
Palacio de Los Matrimonios de La Habana Vieja (Marriage Licensing Bureau), 168
Palacio del Segundo Cabo, 24, *25*, 29

Palacio Presidencial, 156, 186, *187*
Pan-American Conference, 131
El Panchín, 229
Panteon de los Estudiantes (Vilalta de Saavedra), *95, 95, 96* (detail)
Panthéon, Paris, 138
Parajón, Saturnino, 169
Parque Central (Central Park), *10*, 129, 135, 139–40, *143, 144, 146*, 146, *147, 156–59*, 161
Parque de Colón (Columbus Park), *126*, 131
Parque de la Fraternidad Americana (Park of Pan-American Fraternity), *67, 68*, 123, *126–28*, 131, *132–35*, 135, *137*, 139, 146
Parque en el Reparto Miramar (Miramar Park), *220*
Parque Maceo, 186
Parque Martí, 186
Parque y Monumento a Maceo, *189, 190–91* (detail)
Parroquial Mayor. *See* Iglesia Parroquial Mayor
Paseo *192*, 207
Paseo de Martí, 161
Paseo del Prado, 121, 139, 157, *158*, 161, *162–75*, 165, 167, 169, 174, 177, *184*
Paulist Fathers, 87
Pedro Estevez house, *166*, 167
Pedroso family, 150, 154
Peets, Elbert, 186, 192
Pérez, Esley, *10*
Picasso, Pablo, 184
Pinar del Río, 229
Platt Amendment, 121
Playa, 217, 227, 228, 230, 231
La Playa, 223, 228–29
Las Playas bathing pool, 192
Playas de Marianao (Marianao beaches), 222, *226*, 228
Plaza de Albear, 103, *108, 109* (detail)
Plaza de Armas, 7, 19, *22*, 24, *25–28, 36, 37*, 114
Plaza de la Catedral (Cathedral Plaza), *70, 71, 72–77*, 73, *75, 79*, 114
Plaza de San Francisco, 24, *53, 54*, 55–56, *56–69*, 65–66, 133
Plaza Finlay, 217
Plaza Hotel. *See* Hotel Plaza
Plaza Nueva, 24
Plaza Vieja, *113*, 114, *116*
Plazuela de la Ciénaga, 24, 71
Pogolotti, 230
Politeama Building, *144*
Post Office, *56, 58*
postcards, 9–10
Pote's Bridge. *See* Puente de Pote
El Prado. *See* Paseo del Prado
Presbyterians, 88
Presidential Palace. *See* Palacio Presidencial
Primera Avenida (First Avenue), 197
Produce Exchange. *See* Lonja de Comercio
El Progreso bathing pool, 192, 212
Protestantism, 81, 88
Puente Almendares, *227*, 229

Puente de Asbert. *See* Puente Almendares
Puente de Ibañez, 229
Puente de La Lisa, 221
Puente de Línea, 229
Puente de Pote (Pote's Bridge), *197*, 229
Puentes Grandes, 221
La Punta, *178*
La Punta fortress. *See* Castillo de la Punta fortress
La Puntilla, 230
Purdy & Henderson, 136, 156, 215

Los Quemados, 220, 221, 230
Querejeta, 230
Querol, Agustín, Fireman Monument, *97*, 97
Querol, Ramón, 84
Quinta Avenida (Fifth Avenue), 197, *216*, 229

Radiocentro, 215
Rafecas & Tonarely, 195
Ramblas, Barcelona, 174
Ramírez Ovando, Francisco, 188
La Rampa, 215
Rayneri, Eugenio, Jr., 139
Rayneri, Eugenio, Sr., 139
Renaissance style, 13
Reparto Almendares, 228
Reparto de las Murallas (Walls District), 103
Republic. See *La Estatua de la República*
Residencia del Ministro Americano, *230*
La Reunión pharmacy, 112
Revilla de Camargo, Countess, 215
Ringling Bros. and Barnum & Bailey Circus, 195
Río Almendares, *194*, 195, 201, 223
Río Quibú, 217, 221, 223, 229, 231
Rococo style, 88
Roda, Cristóbal de, 177
Roig de Leuchsenring, Emilio, 29
El Romerillo, 230
Roque, Jean-François de la, Seigneur de Roberval, 39
royal palm trees, *58*, 131, 135
Ruiz de Pereda, Gaspar, 42
Rumba Palace, 229

Sacred Heart. *See* Iglesia del Sagrado Corazón
Sagrado Corazón de Jesús (Sacred Heart), 90
Salón de los Pasos Perdidos (Hall of Lost Steps), 139, *141*
Salon (Hotel Trotcha), 211
San Fernando de Peñalver, Condes de, 76
San Francisco de Paula. *See* Iglesia de San Francisco de Paula
San Lázaro Cove, 178, 186
San Lázaro Street. *See* Calle San Lázaro
Santa Dorotea de Luna de la Chorrera Fortress, *194*, 195, 201
Santería, 135
Santo Ángel Custodio, 90
Santo Cristo del Buen Viaje Church. *See* Iglesia del Santo Cristo del Buen Viaje
Santos Suárez, 15

Saratoga Hotel, *130*
Sardá, José María, 84
School of Visual Arts, Instituto Superior de Arte, 224
Schultze and Weaver, 169
Siboney, 230
La Sierra, 230
Simón Bolívar Avenue. *See* Avenida Simón Bolívar
Síscara, Juan de, 24
Sociedad Náutica Havana Yacht Club, 223
Solá, Antonia, *King Fernando VII*, 29
Someillán Building, *197*, 197
Sores, Jacques de, 39
Spanish Renaissance style, 7
St. Francis of Assisi Church. *See* Church and Convent of San Francisco de Asis
Statue of Liberty, 131
Students' Tomb. See *Panteon de los Estudiantes* (Vilalta de Saavedra)

Taboada, Daniel, 55
Tacón market, *113*
Tacón, Miguel de, 24, 66
Tanganana Cave, 178
Teatro Auditorium, 213
Teatro Fausto, *167, 169*, 169
Teatro García Lorca, 155
Teatro Payret, 157
Teatro Principal, 221
Teatro Tacón, *152*, 156
Tejeda, Juan de, 40
El Templete (Columbus Memorial Chapel), 24, *30, 31*
Teresa of Calcutta, Mother, 55
Tobias's Gallery. *See* Galería de Tobías
Torre de La Fuerza (Tower of La Fuerza), *23*
Torre, Marqués de la, 161
El Trabajo (Work), *140*
TRANSIMPORT, 219
Trigo, José Domingo, 201
Tropicana Night Club, 220, *225*
Túnel de Línea, 229
Two Brothers bar. *See* Dos Hermanos (Two Brothers) bar

UNEAC (National Union of Cuban Writers and Artists), 204
UNESCO, 15, 79
Union Club, 177, *180, 181*
University of Havana, 207, *214*
U.S. Interests Section, Swiss embassy, *186*, 186
U.S.S. *Maine*, 178, *182, 183*
U.S.S. *Maine* monument, *182, 183, 197*, 206

Valdés, Miguelito, 229
Vasconcelos, Emilio, 35
Vauban, Marquis de, 48
El Vedado, 15, 184, 192, 195, 197, 201, *202–14*, 207–8, 215, 217, 227, 229
Vedado Church. *See* Iglesia del Vedado
Vedado Tennis Club, 195, *205*

Vega, Lazo de la, 83
Velasco, Dionisio, 188
Velasco Palace, 188
Veracruz Christ, 87
Vernay, Jean Baptiste, 30
Versalles, 231
La Vibora, 15
Vilalta de Saavedra, José
    Francisco de Albear statue, *108*
    Janua sum Pacis, 92, *93*, 95
    José Martí statue, *120*, 140, *146*
    Panteon de los Estudiantes, *95*, 95, *96* (detail)

Villa Soberón, José, *Caballero de Paris*, 60
Villanueva, Conde de, 66, 131
Villegas, Eduardo de, 56
Viñas, Padre, 112
La Virtud Tutelar (The Tutelary), *140*
Vista Alegre bar, 178
Vives, Francisco Dionisio, 24

Washington (Hotel Trotcha), 211
Weldon, Felix de, 186
Welles, Sumner, 135
Workers' Social Club, 205

Yacht Club, 228
Yboleón Bosque, Luis, 201

Zamora, 230
Zanelli, Angelo, *La Estatua de la República*, 139, *142*
Zanja Real (Royal Ditch), 71
Zapata, Julio M., Fireman Monument, *97*, 97
Zayas, Alfredo, *125*
Zenea, Juan Clemente, *164*, 165